Curries & Asian Food

Publisher & Creative Director: Nick Wells
Senior Editor: Sarah Goulding
Designer: Mike Spender
With thanks to: Gina Steer

This is a **FLAME TREE** Book

FLAME TREE PUBLISHING
Crabtree Hall, Crabtree Lane
Fulham, London SW6 6TY
United Kingdom
www.flametreepublishing.com

Flame Tree is part of The Foundry Creative Media Company Limited

First published 2006

07 09 10 08
3 5 7 9 10 8 6 4

ISBN-10 184451 523 0
ISBN-13 978 184451 523 3

A copy of the CIP data for this book is available from the British Library.

Printed in China

Curries & Asian Food

Quick and Easy, Proven Recipes

FLAME TREE
PUBLISHING

Contents

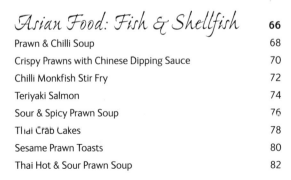

Asian Food: Meat

Asian Food: Poultry

Asian Food: Vegetables & Salads 340

Hygiene in the Kitchen

It is well worth remembering that many foods can carry some form of bacteria. In most cases, the worst it will lead to is a bout of food poisoning or gastroenteritis, although for certain groups this can be more serious. The risk can be reduced or eliminated by good food hygiene and proper cooking.

Do not buy food that is past its sell-by date and do not consume any food that is past its use-by date. When buying food, use the eyes and nose. If the food looks tired, limp or a bad colour or it has a rank, acrid or simply bad smell, do not buy or eat it under any circumstances.

Regularly clean, defrost and clear out the refrigerator or freezer – it is worth checking the packaging to see exactly how long each product is safe to freeze.

Dish cloths and tea towels must be washed and changed regularly. Ideally use disposable cloths which should be replaced on a daily basis. More durable cloths should be left

to soak in bleach, then washed in the washing machine on a boil wash.

Always keep your hands, cooking utensils and food preparation surfaces clean and never allow pets to climb on to any work surfaces.

Buying

Avoid bulk buying where possible, especially fresh produce such as meat, poultry, fish, fruit and vegetables unless buying for the freezer. Fresh foods lose their nutritional value rapidly so buying a little at a time minimises loss of nutrients. It also eliminates a packed refrigerator which reduces the effectiveness of the refrigeration process.

When buying frozen foods, ensure that they are not heavily iced on the outside. Place in the freezer as soon as possible after purchase.

Preparation

Make sure that all work surfaces and utensils are clean and dry. Separate chopping boards should be used for raw and cooked meats, fish and vegetables. It is worth washing all fruits and vegetables regardless of whether they are going to be eaten raw or lightly cooked. Do not reheat food more than once.

All poultry must be thoroughly thawed before cooking. Leave the food in the refrigerator until it is completely thawed. Once defrosted, the chicken should be cooked as soon as possible. The only time food can be refrozen is when the food has been thoroughly thawed then cooked. Once the food has cooled then it can be frozen again for one month.

All poultry and game (except for duck) must be cooked

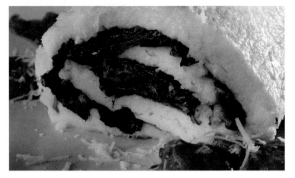

thoroughly. When cooked the juices will run clear. Other meats, like minced meat and pork should be cooked right the way through. Fish should turn opaque, be firm in texture and break easily into large flakes.

Storing, Refrigerating and Freezing

Meat, poultry, fish, seafood and dairy products should all be refrigerated. The temperature of the refrigerator should be between 1–5°C/34–41°F while the freezer temperature should not rise above -18°C/-0.4°F. When refrigerating cooked food, allow it to cool down quickly and completely before refrigerating. Hot food will raise the temperature of the refrigerator and possibly affect or spoil other food stored in it.

Food within the refrigerator and freezer should always be covered. Raw and cooked food should be stored in separate parts of the refrigerator. Cooked food should be kept on the top shelves of the refrigerator, while raw meat, poultry and fish should be placed on bottom shelves to avoid drips and cross-contamination.

High-Risk Foods

Certain foods may carry risks to people who are considered vulnerable such as the elderly, the ill, pregnant women, babies and those suffering from a recurring illness. It is advisable to avoid those foods which belong to a higher-risk category.

There is a slight chance that some eggs carry the bacteria salmonella. Cook the eggs until both the yolk and the white are firm to eliminate this risk. Sauces including Hollandaise, mayonnaise, mousses, soufflés and meringues all use raw or lightly cooked eggs, as do custard-based dishes, ice creams and sorbets. These are all considered high-risk foods to the vulnerable groups mentioned above. Certain meats and poultry also carry the potential risk of salmonella and so should be cooked thoroughly until the juices run clear and there is no pinkness left. Unpasteurised products such as milk, cheese (especially soft cheese), pâté, meat (both raw and cooked) all have the potential risk of listeria and should be avoided.

When buying seafood, buy from a reputable source. Fish should have bright clear eyes, shiny skin and bright pink or red gills. The fish should feel stiff to the touch, with a slight smell of sea air and iodine. The flesh of fish steaks and fillets should be translucent with no signs of discolouration. Avoid any molluscs that are open or do not close when tapped lightly. Univalves such as cockles or winkles should withdraw into their shells when lightly prodded. Squid and octopus should have firm flesh and a pleasant sea smell.

Care is required when freezing seafood. It is imperative to check whether the fish has been frozen before. If it has been, then it should not be frozen again under any circumstances.

Nutrition
The Role of Essential Nutrients

A healthy and well-balanced diet is the body's primary energy source. In children, it constitutes the building blocks for future health as well as providing lots of energy. In adults, it encourages self-healing and regeneration within the body. A well-balanced diet will provide the body with all the essential nutrients it needs. This can be achieved by eating a variety of foods, demonstrated in the pyramid below:

Fats

milk, yogurt
and cheese

Proteins

meat, fish, poultry, eggs,
nuts and pulses

*Fruits and
Vegetables*

Starchy Carbohydrates

cereals, potatoes, bread, rice and pasta

Fats

Fats fall into two categories: saturated and unsaturated fats. It is very important that a healthy balance is achieved within the diet. Fats are an essential part of the diet and a source of energy and provide essential fatty acids and fat soluble vitamins. The right balance of fats should boost the body's immunity to infection and keep muscles, nerves and arteries in good condition. Saturated fats are of animal origin and are hard when stored at room temperature. They can be found in dairy produce, meat, eggs, margarines and hard white cooking fat (lard) as well as in manufactured products such as pies, biscuits and cakes. A high intake of saturated fat over many years has been proven to increase heart disease and high blood cholesterol levels and often leads to weight gain. The aim of a healthy diet is to keep the fat content low in the foods that we eat. Lowering the amount of saturated fat that we consume is very important, but this does not mean that it is good to consume lots of other types of fat.

There are two kinds of unsaturated fats: poly-unsaturated fats and monounsaturated fats. Poly-unsaturated fats include the following oils: safflower oil, soybean oil, corn oil and sesame oil. Within the poly-unsaturated group are Omega oils. The Omega-3 oils are of significant interest because they have been found to be particularly beneficial to coronary health and can encourage brain growth and development. Omega-3 oils are derived from oily fish such as salmon, mackerel, herring, pilchards and sardines. It is recommended that we should eat these types of fish at least once a week. However, for those who do not eat fish or who are vegetarians, liver oil supplements are available in most supermarkets and health shops. It is suggested that these supplements should be taken on a daily basis. The most popular oils that are high in monounsaturates are olive oil, sunflower oil and peanut oil. The Mediterranean diet, which is based on a diet high in mono-unsaturated fats, is recommended for heart health. Also, monounsaturated fats are known to help reduce the levels of LDL (the bad) cholestrol.

Proteins

Composed of amino acids (proteins' building bricks), proteins perform a wide variety of essential functions for the body including supplying energy and building and repairing tissues. Good sources of proteins are eggs, milk, yogurt, cheese, meat, fish, poultry, eggs, nuts and pulses. (See the second level of the pyramid.) Some of these foods, however, contain saturated fats. To strike a nutritional balance eat generous amounts of vegetable protein foods such as soya, beans, lentils, peas and nuts.

Fruits and Vegetables

Not only are fruits and vegetables the most visually appealing foods, but they are extremely good for us, providing essential vitamins and minerals essential for growth, repair and protection in the human body. Fruits and vegetables are low in calories and

are responsible for regulating the body's metabolic processes and controlling the composition of its fluids and cells.

Minerals

CALCIUM Important for healthy bones and teeth, nerve transmission, muscle contraction, blood clotting and hormone function. Calcium promotes a healthy heart, improves skin, relieves aching muscles and bones, maintains the correct acid-alkaline balance and reduces menstrual cramps. Good sources are dairy products, small bones of small fish, nuts, pulses, fortified white flours, breads and green leafy vegetables.

CHROMIUM Part of the glucose tolerance factor, chromium balances blood sugar levels, helps to normalise hunger and reduce cravings, improves lifespan, helps protect DNA and is essential for heart function. Good sources are brewer's yeast, wholemeal bread, rye bread, oysters, potatoes, green peppers, butter and parsnips.

IODINE Important for the manufacture of thyroid hormones and for normal development. Good sources of iodine are seafood, seaweed, milk and dairy products.

IRON As a component of haemoglobin, iron carries oxygen around the body. It is vital for normal growth and development. Good sources are liver, corned beef, red meat, fortified breakfast cereals, pulses, green leafy vegetables, egg yolk and cocoa and cocoa products.

MAGNESIUM Important for efficient functioning of metabolic enzymes and development of the skeleton. Magnesium promotes healthy muscles by helping them to relax and is therefore good for PMS. It is also important for heart muscles and the nervous system. Good sources are nuts, green vegetables, meat, cereals, milk and yogurt.

PHOSPHORUS Forms and maintains bones and teeth, builds muscle tissue, helps maintain the body's pH and aids metabolism and energy production. Phosphorus is present in almost all foods.

POTASSIUM Enables nutrients to move into cells, while waste products move out; promotes healthy nerves and muscles; maintains fluid balance in the body; helps secretion of insulin for blood sugar control to produce constant energy; relaxes muscles; maintains heart functioning and stimulates gut movement to encourage proper elimination. Good sources are fruit, vegetables, milk and bread.

SELENIUM Antioxidant properties help to protect against free radicals and carcinogens. Selenium reduces inflammation, stimulates the immune system to fight infections, promotes a healthy heart and helps vitamin E's action. It is also required for the male reproductive system and is needed for metabolism. Good sources are tuna, liver, kidney, meat, eggs, cereals, nuts and dairy products.

SODIUM Important in helping to control body fluid and balance, preventing dehydration. Sodium is involved in muscle and nerve function and helps move nutrients into cells. All foods are good sources, however processed, pickled and salted foods are richest in sodium.

ZINC Important for metabolism and the healing of wounds. It also aids ability to cope with stress, promotes a healthy nervous system and brain especially in the growing foetus, aids bones and teeth formation and is essential for constant energy. Good sources are liver, meat, pulses, whole-grain cereals, nuts and oysters.

Vitamins

VITAMIN A Important for cell growth and development and for the formation of visual pigments in the eye. Vitamin A comes in two forms: retinol and beta-carotenes. Retinol is found in liver, meat and meat products and whole milk and its products. Beta-carotene is a powerful antioxidant and is found in red and yellow fruits and vegetables such as carrots, mangoes and apricots.

VITAMIN B1 Important in releasing energy from carboydrate-containing foods. Good sources are yeast and yeast products, bread, fortified breakfast cereals and potatoes.

VITAMIN B2 Important for metabolism of proteins, fats and carbohydrates to produce energy. Good sources are meat, yeast extracts, fortified breakfast cereals and milk and its products.

VITAMIN B3 Required for the metabolism of food into energy production. Good sources are milk and milk products, fortified breakfast cereals, pulses, meat, poultry and eggs.

VITAMIN B5 Important for the metabolism of food and energy production. All foods are good sources but especially fortified breakfast cereals, whole-grain bread and dairy products.

VITAMIN B6 Important for metabolism of protein and fat. Vitamin B6 may also be involved with the regulation of sex hormones. Good sources are liver, fish, pork, soya beans and peanuts.

VITAMIN B12 Important for the production of red blood cells and DNA. It is vital for growth and the nervous system. Good sources are meat, fish, eggs, poultry and milk.

BIOTIN Important for metabolism of fatty acids. Good sources of biotin are liver, kidney, eggs and nuts. Micro-organisms also manufacture this vitamin in the gut.

VITAMIN C Important for healing wounds and the formation of collagen which keeps skin and bones strong. It is an important antioxidant. Good sources are fruits, soft summer fruits and vegetables.

VITAMIN D Important for absorption and handling of calcium to help build bone strength. Good sources are oily fish, eggs, whole milk and milk products, margarine and of course sufficient exposure to sunlight, as vitamin D is made in the skin.

VITAMIN E Important as an antioxidant vitamin helping to protect cell membranes from damage. Good sources are vegetable oils, margarines, seeds, nuts and green vegetables.

FOLIC ACID Critical during pregnancy for the development of the brain and nerves. It is always essential for brain and nerve function and is needed for utilising protein and red blood cell formation. Good sources are whole-grain cereals, fortified breakfast cereals, green leafy vegetables, oranges and liver.

VITAMIN K Important for controlling blood clotting. Good sources are cauliflower, Brussels sprouts, lettuce, cabbage, beans, broccoli, peas, asparagus, potatoes, corn oil, tomatoes and milk.

Carbohydrates

Carbohydrates are an energy source and come in two forms: starch and sugar carbohydrates. Starch carbohydrates are also known as complex carbohydrates and they include all cereals, potatoes, breads, rice and pasta. (See the fourth level of the pyramid). Eating whole-grain varieties of these foods also provides fibre. Diets high in fibre are believed to be beneficial in helping to prevent bowel cancer and can also keep cholesterol down. High-fibre diets are also good for those concerned about weight gain. Fibre is bulky so fills the stomach, therefore reducing hunger pangs. Sugar carbohydrates, which are also known as fast-release carbohydrates (because of the quick fix of energy they give to the body), include sugar and sugar-sweetened products such as jams and syrups. Milk provides lactose, which is a milk sugar, and fruits provide fructose, which is a fruit sugar.

Curries

Coconut Fish Curry

SERVES 4

2 tbsp sunflower oil
1 medium onion, peeled
  and very finely chopped
1 yellow pepper, deseeded
  and finely chopped
1 garlic clove, peeled
  and crushed
1 tbsp mild curry paste
2.5 cm/1 inch piece of root
  ginger, peeled and grated

1 red chilli, deseeded
  and finely chopped
400 ml can coconut milk
700 g/1½ lb firm white fish,
  e.g. monkfish fillets,
  skinned and cut into chunks
225 g/8 oz basmati rice
1 tbsp freshly chopped
  coriander
1 tbsp mango chutney

salt and freshly ground
  black pepper

To garnish:
lime wedges
fresh coriander sprigs

To serve:
Greek yogurt
warm naan bread

Put 1 tablespoon of the oil into a large frying pan and cook the onion, pepper and garlic for 5 minutes, or until soft. Add the remaining oil, curry paste, ginger and chilli and cook for a further minute.

Pour in the coconut milk and bring to the boil, reduce the heat and simmer gently for 5 minutes, stirring occasionally. Add the monkfish to the pan and continue to simmer gently for 5–10 minutes, or until the fish is tender, but not overcooked.

Meanwhile, cook the rice in a saucepan of boiling salted water for 15 minutes, or until tender. Drain the rice thoroughly and turn out into a serving dish.

Stir the chopped coriander and chutney gently into the fish curry and season to taste with salt and pepper. Spoon the fish curry over the cooked rice, garnish with lime wedges and coriander sprigs and serve immediately with spoonfuls of Greek yogurt and warm naan bread.

Try this: FOR AN ALTERNATIVE: 356   FOR ENTERTAINING: 292

Red Prawn Curry with Jasmine–scented Rice

SERVES 4

½ tbsp coriander seeds
1 tsp cumin seeds
1 tsp black peppercorns
½ tsp salt
1–2 dried red chillies
2 shallots, peeled and chopped
3–4 garlic cloves
2.5 cm/1 inch piece fresh galangal or root ginger, peeled and chopped
1 kaffir lime leaf or 1 tsp

kaffir lime rind
½ tsp red chilli powder
½ tbsp shrimp paste
1–1½ lemon grass stalks, outer leaves removed and thinly sliced
750 ml/1¼ pints coconut milk
1 red chilli deseeded and thinly sliced
2 tbsp Thai fish sauce
2 tsp soft brown sugar

1 red pepper, deseeded and thinly sliced
550 g/1¼ lb large peeled tiger prawns
2 fresh lime leaves, shredded (optional)
2 tbsp fresh mint leaves, shredded
2 tbsp Thai or Italian basil leaves, shredded
freshly cooked Thai fragrant rice, to serve

Using a pestle and mortar or a spice grinder, grind the coriander and cumin seeds, peppercorns and salt to a fine powder. Add the dried chillies one at a time and grind to a fine powder.

Place the shallots, garlic, galangal or ginger, kaffir lime leaf or rind, chilli powder and shrimp paste in a food processor. Add the ground spices and process until a thick paste forms. Scrape down the bowl once or twice, adding a few drops of water if the mixture is too thick and not forming a paste. Stir in the lemon grass.

Transfer the paste to a large wok and cook over a medium heat for 2–3 minutes or until fragrant. Stir in the coconut milk, bring to the boil, then lower the heat and simmer for about 10 minutes. Add the chilli, fish sauce, sugar and red pepper and simmer for 15 minutes.

Stir in the prawns and cook for 5 minutes, or until the prawns are pink and tender. Stir in the shredded herbs, heat for a further minute and serve immediately with the cooked rice.

Try this: FOR AN ALTERNATIVE: 36   FOR ENTERTAINING: 82

Thai Curried Seafood

SERVES 6-8

2 tbsp vegetable oil
450 g/1 lb scallops, with coral attached if preferred, halved if large
1 onion, peeled and finely chopped
4 garlic cloves, peeled and finely chopped
5 cm/2 inch piece fresh root ginger, peeled and finely chopped
1–2 red chillies, deseeded and thinly sliced
1–2 tbsp curry paste (hot or medium, to taste)
1 tsp ground coriander
1 tsp ground cumin
1 lemon grass stalk, bruised
225 g can chopped tomatoes
125 ml/4 fl oz chicken stock or water
450 ml/¾ pint coconut milk
12 live mussels, scrubbed and beards removed
450 g/1 lb cooked peeled prawns
225 g/8 oz frozen or canned crabmeat, drained
2 tbsp freshly chopped coriander
freshly shredded coconut, to garnish (optional)
freshly cooked rice or rice noodles, to serve

Heat a wok or large frying pan, add 1 tablespoon of the oil and when hot, add the scallops and stir-fry for 2 minutes or until opaque and firm. Transfer to a plate with any juices.

Heat the remaining oil. Add the onion, garlic, ginger and chillies and stir-fry for 1 minute or until they begin to soften.

Add the curry paste, coriander, cumin and lemon grass and stir-fry for 2 minutes. Add the tomatoes and stock, bring to the boil then simmer for 5 minutes or until reduced, stirring constantly. Stir in the coconut milk and simmer for 2 minutes.

Stir in the mussels, cover and simmer for 2 minutes or until they begin to open. Stir in the prawns, crabmeat and reserved scallops with any juices and cook for 2 minutes or until heated through. Discard the lemon grass and any unopened mussels. Stir in the chopped coriander. Tip into a large warmed serving dish and garnish with the coconut, if using. Serve immediately with rice or noodles.

Try this: FOR AN ALTERNATIVE: 96   FOR ENTERTAINING: 116

Lobster & Prawn Curry

SERVES 4

225 g/8 oz cooked lobster meat, shelled if necessary
225 g/8 oz raw tiger prawns, peeled and de-veined
2 tbsp groundnut oil
2 bunches spring onions, trimmed and thickly sliced

2 garlic cloves, peeled and chopped
2.5 cm/1 inch piece fresh root ginger, peeled and cut into matchsticks
2 tbsp Thai red curry paste
grated zest and juice of 1 lime

200 ml/7 fl oz coconut cream
salt and freshly ground black pepper
3 tbsp freshly chopped coriander
freshly cooked Thai fragrant rice, to serve

Using a sharp knife, slice the lobster meat thickly. Wash the tiger prawns and pat dry with absorbent kitchen paper. Make a small 1 cm/½ inch cut at the tail end of each prawn and reserve.

Heat a large wok, then add the oil and, when hot, stir-fry the lobster and tiger prawns for 4–6 minutes, or until pink. Using a slotted spoon, transfer to a plate and keep warm in a low oven.

Add the spring onions and stir-fry for 2 minutes, then stir in the garlic and ginger and stir-fry for a further 2 minutes. Add the curry paste and stir-fry for 1 minute.

Pour in the coconut cream, lime zest and juice and the seasoning. Bring to the boil and simmer for 1 minute. Return the prawns and lobster and any juices to the wok and simmer for 2 minutes. Stir in two thirds of the freshly chopped coriander to the wok mixture, then sprinkle with the remaining coriander and serve immediately.

Try this: FOR AN ALTERNATIVE: 84   FOR ENTERTAINING: 140

Thai Coconut Crab Curry

SERVES 4-6

1 onion
4 garlic cloves
5 cm/2 inch piece fresh
    root ginger
2 tbsp vegetable oil
2–3 tsp hot curry paste

400 g/14 oz coconut milk
2 large dressed crabs, white
    and dark meat separated
2 lemon grass stalks, peeled
    and bruised
6 spring onions, trimmed

and chopped
2 tbsp freshly shredded
    Thai basil or mint, plus
    extra, to garnish
freshly boiled rice,
    to serve

Peel the onion and chop finely. Peel the garlic cloves, then either crush or finely chop. Peel the ginger and either grate coarsely or cut into very thin shreds. Reserve.

Heat a wok or large frying pan, add the oil and when hot, add the onion, garlic and ginger and stir-fry for 2 minutes, or until the onion is beginning to soften. Stir in the curry paste and stir-fry for 1 minute.

Stir the coconut milk into the vegetable mixture with the dark crabmeat. Add the lemon grass, then bring the mixture slowly to the boil, stirring frequently.

Add the spring onions and simmer gently for 15 minutes or until the sauce has thickened. Remove and discard the lemon grass stalks.

Add the white crabmeat and the shredded basil or mint and stir very gently for 1–2 minutes or until heated through and piping hot. Try to prevent the crabmeat from breaking up.

Spoon the curry over boiled rice on warmed individual plates, sprinkle with basil or mint leaves and serve immediately.

Try this: FOR AN ALTERNATIVE: 164   FOR ENTERTAINING: 128

Green Chicken Curry

SERVES 4

1 onion, peeled and chopped
3 lemon grass stalks, outer leaves discarded and finely sliced
2 garlic cloves, peeled and finely chopped
1 tbsp freshly grated

root ginger
3 green chillies
zest and juice of 1 lime
2 tbsp groundnut oil
2 tbsp Thai fish sauce
6 tbsp freshly chopped coriander
6 tbsp freshly chopped basil

450 g/1 lb skinless, boneless chicken breasts, cut into strips
125 g /4 oz fine green beans, trimmed
400 ml can coconut milk
fresh basil leaves, to garnish
freshly cooked rice, to serve

Place the onion, lemon grass, garlic, ginger, chillies, lime zest and juice, 1 tablespoon of groundnut oil, the fish sauce, coriander and basil in a food processor. Blend to a form a smooth paste, which should be of a spoonable consistency. If the sauce looks thick, add a little water. Remove and reserve.

Heat the wok, add the remaining 1 tablespoon of oil and when hot add the chicken. Stir-fry for 2–3 minutes, until the chicken starts to colour, then add the green beans and stir-fry for a further minute. Remove the chicken and beans from the wok and reserve. Wipe the wok clean with absorbent kitchen paper.

Spoon the reserved green paste into the wok and heat for 1 minute. Add the coconut milk and whisk to blend. Return the chicken and beans to the wok and bring to the boil. Simmer for 5–7 minutes, or until the chicken is cooked. Sprinkle with basil leaves and serve immediately with freshly cooked rice.

Try this: FOR AN ALTERNATIVE: 36 FOR ENTERTAINING: 276

Aromatic Chicken Curry

SERVES 4

125 g/4 oz red lentils
2 tsp ground coriander
½ tsp cumin seeds
2 tsp mild curry paste
1 bay leaf
small strip of lemon rind
600 ml/1 pint chicken or

vegetable stock
8 chicken thighs, skinned
175 g/6 oz spinach leaves,
  rinsed and shredded
1 tbsp freshly
  chopped coriander
2 tsp lemon juice

salt and freshly ground
  black pepper

To serve:
freshly cooked rice
natural yogurt

Put the lentils in a sieve and rinse thoroughly under cold running water.

Dry-fry the ground coriander and cumin seeds in a large saucepan over a low heat for about 30 seconds. Stir in the curry paste.

Add the lentils to the saucepan with the bay leaf and lemon rind, then pour in the stock. Stir, then slowly bring to the boil. Turn down the heat, half-cover the pan with a lid and simmer gently for 5 minutes, stirring occasionally.

Secure the chicken thighs with cocktail sticks to keep their shape. Place in the pan and half cover. Simmer for 15 minutes.

Stir in the shredded spinach and cook for a further 25 minutes or until the chicken is very tender and the sauce is thick.

Remove the bay leaf and lemon rind. Stir in the coriander and lemon juice, then season to taste with salt and pepper. Serve immediately with the rice and a little natural yogurt.

Try this: FOR AN ALTERNATIVE: 256   FOR ENTERTAINING: 280

Creamy Chicken & Rice Pilau

SERVES 4-6

350 g/12 oz basmati rice
salt and freshly ground
   black pepper
50 g/2 oz butter
100 g/3½ oz flaked almonds
75 g/3 oz unsalted shelled
   pistachio nuts
4–6 skinless chicken
   breast fillets, each cut
   into 4 pieces

2 tbsp vegetable oil
2 medium onions, peeled
   and thinly sliced
2 garlic cloves, peeled
   and finely chopped
2.5 cm/1 inch piece of fresh
   root ginger, finely chopped
6 green cardamom pods,
   lightly crushed
4–6 whole cloves

2 bay leaves
1 tsp ground coriander
½ tsp cayenne pepper,
   or to taste
225 ml/8 fl oz natural yogurt
225 ml/8 fl oz double cream
225 g/8 oz seedless green
   grapes, halved if large
2 tbsp freshly chopped
   coriander or mint

Bring a saucepan of lightly salted water to the boil. Gradually pour in the rice; return to the boil, then simmer for about 12 minutes until tender. Drain, rinse under cold water and reserve.

Heat the butter in a large deep frying pan over a medium-high heat. Add the almonds and pistachios and cook for about 2 minutes, stirring constantly, until golden. Using a slotted spoon, transfer to a plate. Add the chicken pieces to the pan and cook for 5 minutes, or until golden, turning once. Remove from the pan and reserve. Add the oil to the pan and cook the onions for 10 minutes, or until golden, stirring frequently. Stir in the garlic, ginger and spices and cook for 2–3 minutes, stirring. Add 2–3 tablespoons of the yogurt and cook, stirring until the moisture evaporates. Continue adding the yogurt in this way until it is used up.

Return the chicken and nuts to the pan and stir. Stir in 125 ml/4 fl oz of boiling water and season to taste with salt and pepper. Cook, covered, over a low heat for 10 minutes until the chicken is tender. Stir in the cream, grapes and half the herbs. Gently fold in the rice. Heat through for 5 minutes and sprinkle with the remaining herbs, then serve.

Try this: FOR AN ALTERNATIVE: 272 FOR ENTERTAINING: 290

Persian Chicken Pilaf

SERVES 4-6

2–3 tbsp vegetable oil
700 g/1½ lb boneless,
  skinless chicken pieces
  (breast and thighs),
  cut into 2.5 cm/
  1 inch pieces
2 medium onions, peeled
  and coarsely chopped
1 tsp ground cumin

200 g/7 oz long-grain
  white rice
1 tbsp tomato purée
1 tsp saffron strands
salt and freshly ground
  black pepper
100 ml/3½ fl oz
  pomegranate juice
900 ml/1½ pints

chicken stock
125 g/4 oz ready-to-eat dried
  apricots or prunes, halved
2 tbsp raisins
2 tbsp freshly chopped
  mint or parsley
pomegranate seeds, to
  garnish (optional)

Heat the oil in a large heavy-based saucepan over a medium-high heat. Cook the chicken pieces, in batches, until lightly browned. Return all the browned chicken to the saucepan.

Add the onions to the saucepan, reduce the heat to medium and cook for 3–5 minutes, stirring frequently, until the onions begin to soften. Add the cumin and rice and stir to coat the rice. Cook for about 2 minutes until the rice is golden and translucent. Stir in the tomato purée and the saffron strands, then season to taste with salt and pepper.

Add the pomegranate juice and stock and bring to the boil, stirring once or twice. Add the apricots or prunes and raisins and stir gently. Reduce the heat to low and cook for 30 minutes until the chicken and rice are tender and the liquid is absorbed.

Turn into a shallow serving dish and sprinkle with the chopped mint or parsley. Serve immediately, garnished with pomegranate seeds, if using.

Try this: FOR AN ALTERNATIVE: 286   FOR ENTERTAINING: 262

Red Chicken Curry

SERVES 4

225 ml/8 fl oz coconut cream
2 tbsp vegetable oil
2 garlic clove, peeled and
   finely chopped
2 tbsp Thai red curry paste
2 tbsp Thai fish sauce

2 tsp sugar
350 g/12 oz boneless,
   skinless chicken breast,
   finely sliced
450 ml/¾ pint chicken stock
2 lime leaves, shredded

chopped red chilli,
   to garnish
freshly boiled rice or
   steamed Thai fragrant
   rice, to serve

Pour the coconut cream into a small saucepan and heat gently. Meanwhile, heat a wok or large frying pan and add the oil. When the oil is very hot, swirl the oil around the wok until the wok is lightly coated, then add the garlic and stir-fry for about 10–20 seconds, or until the garlic begins to brown. Add the curry paste and stir-fry for a few more seconds, then pour in the warmed coconut cream.

Cook the coconut cream mixture for 5 minutes, or until the cream has curdled and thickened. Stir in the fish sauce and sugar. Add the finely sliced chicken breast and cook for 3–4 minutes, or until the chicken has turned white.

Pour the stock into the wok, bring to the boil, then simmer for 1–2 minutes, or until the chicken is cooked through. Stir in the shredded lime leaves. Turn into a warmed serving dish, garnish with chopped red chilli and serve immediately with rice.

Try this: FOR AN ALTERNATIVE: 28   FOR ENTERTAINING: 294

Chicken & Red Pepper Curried Rice

SERVES 4

350 g/12 oz long-grain rice
salt to taste
1 large egg white
1 tbsp cornflour
300 g/11 oz skinless
   chicken breast fillets,

cut into chunks
3 tbsp groundnut oil
1 red pepper, deseeded and
   roughly chopped
1 tbsp curry powder or paste
125 ml/4 fl oz chicken stock

1 tsp sugar
1 tbsp Chinese rice wine
   or dry sherry
1 tbsp light soy sauce
sprigs of fresh
   coriander, to garnish

Wash the rice in several changes of water until the water remains relatively clear. Drain well. Put into a saucepan and cover with fresh water. Add a little salt and bring to the boil. Cook for 7–8 minutes until tender. Drain and refresh under cold running water, then drain again and reserve.

Lightly whisk the egg white with 1 teaspoon of salt and 2 teaspoons of cornflour until smooth. Add the chicken and mix together well. Cover and chill in the refrigerator for 20 minutes.

Heat the oil in a wok until moderately hot. Add the chicken mixture to the wok and stir-fry for 2–3 minutes until all the chicken has turned white. Using a slotted spoon, lift the cubes of chicken from the wok, then drain on absorbent kitchen paper.

Add the red pepper to the wok and stir-fry for 1 minute over a high heat. Add the curry powder or paste and cook for a further 30 seconds, then add the chicken stock, sugar, Chinese rice wine and soy sauce. Mix the remaining cornflour with 1 teaspoon of cold water and add to the wok, stirring. Bring to the boil and simmer gently for 1 minute.

Return the chicken to the wok, then simmer for a further 1 minute before adding the rice. Stir over a medium heat for another 2 minutes until heated through. Garnish with the sprigs of coriander and serve.

Try this: FOR AN ALTERNATIVE: 236 FOR ENTERTAINING: 266

Chicken Tikka Masala

SERVES 4

4 skinless chicken
    breast fillets
150 ml/¼ pint natural yogurt
1 garlic clove,
    peeled and crushed
2.5 cm/1 inch piece fresh
    root ginger, peeled
    and grated
1 tsp chilli powder

1 tbsp ground coriander
2 tbsp lime juice
twist of lime, to garnish
freshly cooked rice, to serve

For the masala sauce:
15 g/½ oz unsalted butter
2 tbsp sunflower oil
1 onion, peeled

    and chopped
1 green chilli, deseeded and
    finely chopped
1 tsp garam masala
150 ml/¼ pint double cream
salt and freshly ground
    black pepper
3 tbsp fresh coriander
    leaves, roughly torn

Preheat the oven to 200°C/400°F/Gas Mark 6, 15 minutes before cooking. Cut each chicken breast across into three pieces, then make two or three shallow cuts in each piece. Put in a shallow dish. Mix together the yogurt, garlic, ginger, chilli powder, ground coriander and lime juice. Pour over the chicken, cover and marinate in the refrigerator for up to 24 hours.

Remove the chicken from the marinade and arrange on an oiled baking tray. Bake in the preheated oven for 15 minutes, or until golden brown and cooked.

While the chicken is cooking, heat the butter and oil in a wok and stir-fry the onion for 5 minutes, or until tender. Add the chilli and garam masala and stir-fry for a few more seconds. Stir in the cream and remaining marinade. Simmer over a low heat for 1 minute, stirring all the time.

Add the chicken pieces and cook for a further 1 minute, stirring to coat in the sauce. Season to taste with salt and pepper. Transfer the chicken pieces to a warmed serving plate. Stir the chopped coriander into the sauce, then spoon over the chicken, garnish and serve immediately with freshly cooked rice.

Try this: FOR AN ALTERNATIVE: 254   FOR ENTERTAINING: 264

Beef Curry with Lemon & Arborio Rice

SERVES 4

450 g/1 lb beef fillet
1 tbsp olive oil
2 tbsp green curry paste
1 green pepper, deseeded
   and cut into strips
1 red pepper, deseeded

and cut into strips
1 celery stick, trimmed
   and sliced
juice of 1 fresh lemon
2 tsp Thai fish sauce
2 tsp demerara sugar

225 g/8 oz Arborio rice
15 g/ ½ oz butter
2 tbsp freshly
   chopped coriander
4 tbsp crème fraîche

Trim the beef fillet, discarding any fat, then cut across the grain into thin slices. Heat a wok, add the oil and when hot, add the green curry paste and cook for 30 seconds. Add the beef strips and stir-fry for 3–4 minutes.

Add the sliced peppers and the celery and continue to stir-fry for 2 minutes. Add the lemon juice, Thai fish sauce and sugar and cook for a further 3–4 minutes, or until the beef is tender and cooked to personal preference.

Meanwhile, cook the Arborio rice in a saucepan of lightly salted boiling water for 15–20 minutes, or until tender. Drain, rinse with boiling water and drain again. Return to the saucepan and add the butter. Cover and allow the butter to melt before turning it out onto a large serving dish. Sprinkle the cooked curry with the chopped coriander and serve immediately with the rice and crème fraîche.

Try this: FOR AN ALTERNATIVE: 264   FOR ENTERTAINING: 158

Beef & Mushroom Curry

SERVES 4

700 g/1½ lb rump steak
3 tbsp vegetable oil
2 onions, peeled and thinly
sliced into rings
2 garlic cloves, crushed
2.5cm/1 inch piece
ginger root, chopped
2 fresh green chillies,

deseeded and chopped
1 ½ tbsp medium
curry paste
1 tsp ground coriander
350g/12oz long-grain rice
60g/2oz butter
225g/8oz button
mushrooms, wiped

and sliced
900 ml/1½ pints stock
3 tomatoes, chopped
salt and freshly ground
black pepper
60g/2oz creamed coconut,
chopped
2 tbsp ground almonds

Beat the steak until very thin, then trim off and discard the fat and cut into thin strips. Heat the oil in a saucepan, add the beef and fry until sealed, stirring frequently. Remove beef and place to one side.

Fry the onions, garlic, ginger, chillies, curry paste and coriander for 2 minutes. Add the mushrooms, stock and tomatoes and season to taste.

Return the beef to the pan. Cover the pan and simmer gently for 1 ¼ – 1 ½ hours or until the beef is tender.

Place the rice in a saucepan of boiling salted water, and simmer for 15 minutes until tender or according to the package directions. Drain the rice then return to the saucepan, add the butter, cover and keep warm.

Stir the creamed coconut and ground almonds into the curry, cover the pan and cook gently for 3 minutes. Serve with the rice.

Try this: FOR AN ALTERNATIVE: 164   FOR ENTERTAINING: 170

Spicy Pork

SERVES 4

4 tbsp groundnut oil
2.5 cm/1 inch piece fresh
    root ginger, peeled and
    cut into matchsticks
1 garlic clove, peeled
    and chopped
2 medium carrots, peeled
    and cut into matchsticks

1 medium aubergine,
    trimmed and cubed
700 g/1½ lb pork fillet,
    thickly sliced
400 ml/14 fl oz coconut milk
2 tbsp Thai red curry paste
4 tbsp Thai fish sauce
2 tsp caster sugar

227 g can bamboo shoots in
    brine, drained and cut into
    matchsticks
salt, to taste
lime zest, to garnish
freshly cooked rice,
    to serve

Heat a wok or large frying pan, add 2 tablespoons of the oil and when hot, add the ginger, garlic, carrots and aubergine and stir-fry for 3 minutes. Using a slotted spoon, transfer to a plate and keep warm.

Add the remaining oil to the wok, heat until smoking, then add the pork and stir-fry for 5–8 minutes or until browned all over. Transfer to a plate and keep warm. Wipe the wok clean.

Pour half the coconut milk into the wok, stir in the red curry paste and bring to the boil. Boil rapidly for 4 minutes, stirring occasionally, or until the sauce is reduced by half.

Add the fish sauce and sugar to the wok and bring back to the boil. Return the pork and vegetables to the wok with the bamboo shoots. Return to the boil, then simmer for 4 minutes.

Stir in the remaining coconut milk and season to taste with salt. Simmer for 2 minutes or until heated through. Garnish with lime zest and serve immediately with rice.

Try this: FOR AN ALTERNATIVE: 180   FOR ENTERTAINING: 154

Spicy Cucumber Stir Fry

SERVES 4

25 g/1 oz black soya beans,
soaked in cold water,
overnight
1½ cucumbers
2 tsp salt

1 tbsp groundnut oil
½ tsp mild chilli powder
4 garlic cloves, peeled and
crushed
5 tbsp chicken stock

1 tsp sesame oil
1 tbsp freshly chopped
parsley, to garnish

Rinse the soaked beans thoroughly, then drain. Place in a saucepan, cover with cold water and bring to the boil, skimming off any scum that rises to the surface. Boil for 10 minutes, then reduce the heat and simmer for 1–1 ½ hours. Drain and reserve.

Peel the cucumbers, slice lengthways and remove the seeds. Cut into 2.5 cm/1 inch slices and place in a colander over a bowl. Sprinkle the salt over the cucumber and leave for 30 minutes. Rinse thoroughly in cold water, drain and pat dry with absorbent kitchen paper.

Heat a wok or large frying pan, add the oil and when hot, add the chilli powder, garlic and black beans and stir-fry for 30 seconds. Add the cucumber and stir-fry for 20 seconds.

Pour the stock into the wok and cook for 3–4 minutes, or until the cucumber is very tender. The liquid will have evaporated at this stage. Remove from the heat and stir in the sesame oil. Turn into a warmed serving dish, garnish with chopped parsley and serve immediately.

Try this: FOR AN ALTERNATIVE: 360 FOR ENTERTAINING: 366

Lamb Korma

SERVES 4

1 tsp hot chilli powder
1 tsp ground cinnamon
1 tsp medium hot
   curry powder
1 tsp ground cumin
salt and freshly ground
   black pepper
2 tbsp groundnut oil
450 g/1 lb lamb fillet,
   trimmed

4 cardamom pods, bruised
4 whole cloves
1 onion, peeled and
   finely sliced
2 garlic cloves,
   peeled and crushed
2.5 cm/1 inch piece fresh
   root ginger, peeled
   and grated
150 ml/¼ pint Greek

style yogurt
1 tbsp freshly
   chopped coriander
2 spring onions, trimmed
   and finely sliced

To serve
freshly cooked rice
naan bread

Blend the chilli powder, cinnamon, curry powder, cumin and seasoning with 2 tablespoons of the oil in a bowl and reserve. Cut the lamb fillet into thin strips, add to the spice and oil mixture and stir until coated thoroughly. Cover and leave to marinate in the refrigerator for at least 30 minutes.

Heat the wok, then pour in the remaining oil. When hot, add the cardamom pods and cloves and stir-fry for 10 seconds. Add the onion, garlic and ginger to the wok and stir fry for 3–4 minutes until softened.

Add the lamb with the marinading ingredients and stir-fry for a further 3 minutes until cooked. Pour in the yogurt, stir thoroughly and heat until piping hot. Sprinkle with the chopped coriander and sliced spring onions then serve immediately with freshly cooked rice and naan bread.

Try this: FOR AN ALTERNATIVE: 230 FOR ENTERTAINING: 228

Calypso Rice with Curried Bananas

SERVES 4

2 tbsp sunflower oil
1 medium onion, peeled
and finely chopped
1 garlic clove,
peeled and crushed
1 red chilli, deseeded
and finely chopped
1 red pepper,
deseeded and chopped

225 g/8 oz basmati rice
juice of 1 lime
350 ml/12 fl oz
vegetable stock
200 g can black-eye beans,
drained and rinsed
2 tbsp freshly
chopped parsley
salt and freshly ground

black pepper
sprigs of coriander,
to garnish

For the curried bananas:
4 green bananas
2 tbsp sunflower oil
2 tsp mild curry paste
200 ml/7 fl oz coconut milk

Heat the oil in a large frying pan and gently cook the onion, for 10 minutes until soft. Add the garlic, chilli and red pepper and cook for 2–3 minutes.

Rinse the rice under cold running water, then add to the pan and stir. Pour in the lime juice and stock, bring to the boil, cover and simmer for 12–15 minutes, or until the rice is tender and the stock is absorbed. Stir in the black-eye beans and chopped parsley and season to taste with salt and pepper. Leave to stand, covered, for 5 minutes before serving to allow the beans to warm through.

While the rice is cooking, make the curried green bananas. Remove the skins from the bananas – they may need to be cut off with a sharp knife. Slice the flesh thickly. Heat the oil in a frying pan and cook the bananas, in 2 batches, for 2–3 minutes, or until lightly browned.

Pour the coconut milk into the pan and stir in the curry paste. Add the banana slices to the coconut milk and simmer, uncovered, over a low heat for 8–10 minutes, or until the bananas are very soft and the coconut milk slightly reduced. Spoon the rice onto warmed serving plates, garnish with coriander and serve immediately with the curried bananas.

Try this: FOR AN ALTERNATIVE: 64   FOR ENTERTAINING: 56

Thai–style Cauliflower & Potato Curry

SERVES 4

450 g/1 lb new potatoes, peeled and halved or quartered
350 g/12 oz cauliflower florets
3 garlic cloves, peeled and crushed
1 onion, peeled and finely chopped
40 g/1½ oz ground almonds
1 tsp ground coriander
½ tsp ground cumin
½ tsp turmeric
3 tbsp groundnut oil
salt and freshly ground black pepper
50 g/2 oz creamed coconut, broken into small pieces
200 ml/7 fl oz vegetable stock
1 tbsp mango chutney
sprigs of fresh coriander, to garnish
freshly cooked long-grain rice, to serve

Bring a saucepan of lightly salted water to the boil, add the potatoes and cook for 15 minutes or until just tender. Drain and leave to cool. Boil the cauliflower for 2 minutes, then drain and refresh under cold running water. Drain again and reserve.

Meanwhile, blend the garlic, onion, ground almonds and spices with 2 tablespoons of the oil and salt and pepper to taste in a food processor until a smooth paste is formed. Heat a wok, add the remaining oil and when hot, add the spice paste and cook for 3–4 minutes, stirring continuously.

Dissolve the creamed coconut in 6 tablespoons of boiling water and add to the wok. Pour in the stock, cook for 2–3 minutes, then stir in the cooked potatoes and cauliflower.

Stir in the mango chutney and heat through for 3–4 minutes or until piping hot. Tip into a warmed serving dish, garnish with sprigs of fresh coriander and serve immediately with freshly cooked rice.

Try this: FOR AN ALTERNATIVE: 52   FOR ENTERTAINING: 64

Creamy Vegetable Korma

SERVES 4-6

2 tbsp ghee or vegetable oil
1 large onion, peeled
   and chopped
2 garlic cloves, peeled
   and crushed
2.5 cm/1 inch piece of root
   ginger, peeled and grated
4 cardamom pods
2 tsp ground coriander
1 tsp ground cumin

1 tsp ground turmeric
finely grated rind and juice
   of ½ lemon
50 g/2 oz ground almonds
400 ml/14 fl oz vegetable
   stock
450 g/1 lb potatoes, peeled
   and diced
450 g/1 lb mixed vegetables,
   such as cauliflower,

carrots and turnip,
   cut into chunks
150 ml/¼ pint double cream
3 tbsp freshly
   chopped coriander
salt and freshly ground
   black pepper
naan bread, to serve

Heat the ghee or oil in a large saucepan. Add the onion and cook for 5 minutes. Stir in the garlic and ginger and cook for a further 5 minutes, or until soft and just beginning to colour.

Stir in the cardamom, ground coriander, cumin and turmeric. Continue cooking over a low heat for 1 minute, stirring.

Stir in the lemon rind and juice and almonds. Blend in the vegetable stock. Slowly bring to the boil, stirring occasionally.

Add the potatoes and vegetables. Bring back to the boil, then reduce the heat, cover and simmer for 35–40 minutes, or until the vegetables are just tender. Check after 25 minutes and add a little more stock if needed.

Slowly stir in the cream and chopped coriander. Season to taste with salt and pepper. Cook very gently until heated through, but do not boil. Serve immediately with naan bread.

Try this: FOR AN ALTERNATIVE: 58   FOR ENTERTAINING: 370

Vegetable Kofta Curry

SERVES 6

350 g/12 oz potatoes,
  peeled and diced
225 g/8 oz carrots, peeled
  and roughly chopped
225 g/8 oz parsnips, peeled
  and roughly chopped
1 medium egg, lightly beaten
75 g/3 oz plain flour, sifted
8 tbsp sunflower oil

2 onions, peeled and sliced
2 garlic cloves,
  peeled and crushed
2.5 cm/1 inch piece
  fresh root ginger,
  peeled and grated
2 tbsp garam masala
2 tbsp tomato paste
300 ml/½ pint

vegetable stock
250 ml/9 fl oz Greek
  style yogurt
3 tbsp freshly
  chopped coriander
salt and freshly ground
  black pepper

Bring a saucepan of lightly salted water to the boil. Add the potatoes, carrots and parsnips. Cover and simmer for 12–15 minutes, or until the vegetables are tender. Drain the vegetables and mash until very smooth. Stir the egg into the vegetable purée, then add the flour and mix to make a stiff paste and reserve.

Heat 2 tablespoons of the oil in a wok and gently cook the onions for 10 minutes. Add the garlic and ginger and cook for a further 2–3 minutes, or until very soft and just beginning to colour. Sprinkle the garam masala over the onions and stir in. Add the tomato paste and stock. Bring to the boil, cover and simmer gently for 15 minutes.

Meanwhile, heat the remaining oil in a wok or frying pan. Drop in tablespoons of vegetable batter, four or five at a time and fry, turning often, for 3–4 minutes until brown and crisp. Remove with a slotted spoon and drain on absorbent kitchen paper. Keep warm in a low oven while cooking the rest. Stir the yogurt and coriander into the onion sauce. Slowly heat to boiling point and season to taste with salt and pepper. Divide the koftas between warmed serving plates and spoon over the sauce. Serve immediately.

Try this: FOR AN ALTERNATIVE: 62 FOR ENTERTAINING: 358

Thai Curry with Tofu

SERVES 4

750 ml/1¼ pints
  coconut milk
700 g/1½ lb tofu, drained and
  cut into small cubes
salt and freshly ground
  black pepper
4 garlic cloves,
  peeled and chopped
1 large onion, peeled

and cut into wedges
1 tsp crushed dried chillies
grated rind of 1 lemon
2.5 cm/1 inch piece fresh root
  ginger, peeled and grated
1 tbsp ground coriander
1 tsp ground cumin
1 tsp turmeric
2 tbsp light soy sauce

1 tsp cornflour
Thai fragrant rice, to serve

To garnish:
2 red chillies, deseeded
  and cut into rings
1 tbsp freshly
  chopped coriander
lemon wedges

Pour 600 ml/1 pint of the coconut milk into a saucepan and bring to the boil. Add the tofu, season to taste with salt and pepper and simmer gently for 10 minutes. Using a slotted spoon, remove the tofu and place on a plate. Reserve the coconut milk.

Place the garlic, onion, dried chillies, lemon rind, ginger, spices and soy sauce in a blender or food processor and blend until a smooth paste is formed. Pour the remaining 150 ml/¼ pint coconut milk into a clean saucepan and whisk in the spicy paste. Cook, stirring continuously, for 15 minutes, or until the curry sauce is very thick.

Gradually whisk the reserved coconut milk into the curry and heat to simmering point. Add the cooked tofu and cook for 5–10 minutes. Blend the cornflour with 1 tablespoon of cold water and stir into the curry. Cook until thickened. Turn into a warmed serving dish and garnish with chilli, lemon wedges and coriander. Serve immediately with Thai fragrant rice.

Try this: FOR AN ALTERNATIVE: 366   FOR ENTERTAINING: 364

Vegetable Biryani

SERVES 4

2 tbsp vegetable oil, plus a little extra for brushing
2 large onions, peeled and thinly sliced lengthwise
2 garlic cloves, peeled and finely chopped
2.5 cm/1 inch piece fresh root ginger, peeled and finely grated
1 small carrot, peeled and cut into sticks
1 small parsnip, peeled and diced
1 small sweet potato chunks, peeled and diced
1 tbsp medium curry paste
225 g/8 oz basmati rice
4 ripe tomatoes, peeled, deseeded and diced
600 ml/1 pint vegetable stock
175 g/6 oz cauliflower florets
50 g/2 oz peas, thawed if frozen
salt and freshly ground black pepper

To garnish:
roasted cashew nuts
raisins
fresh coriander leaves

Preheat the oven to 200°C/400°F/Gas Mark 6. Put 1 tablespoon of the vegetable oil in a large bowl with the onions and toss to coat. Lightly brush or spray a non-stick baking sheet with a little more oil. Spread half the onions on the baking sheet and cook at the top of the preheated oven for 25–30 minutes, stirring regularly, until golden and crisp. Remove from the oven and reserve for the garnish.

Meanwhile, heat a large flameproof casserole over a medium heat and add the remaining oil and onions. Cook for 5–7 minutes until softened and starting to brown. Add a little water if they start to stick. Add the garlic and ginger and cook for another minute, then add the carrot, parsnip and sweet potato. Cook the vegetables for a further 5 minutes. Add the curry paste and stir for a minute until everything is coated, then stir in the rice and tomatoes. After 2 minutes add the stock and stir well. Bring to the boil, cover and simmer over a very gentle heat for about 10 minutes.

Add the cauliflower and peas and cook for 8–10 minutes, or until the rice is tender. Season to taste with salt and pepper. Serve garnished with the crispy onions, cashew nuts, raisins and coriander.

Try this: FOR AN ALTERNATIVE: 34 FOR ENTERTAINING: 370

Pumpkin & Chickpea Curry

SERVES 4

1 tbsp vegetable oil
1 small onion,
 peeled and sliced
2 garlic cloves, peeled
 and finely chopped
2.5 cm/1 inch piece root
 ginger, peeled and grated
1 tsp ground coriander
½ tsp ground cumin
½ tsp ground turmeric

¼ tsp ground cinnamon
2 tomatoes, chopped
2 red bird's eye
 chillies, deseeded
 and finely chopped
450 g/1 lb pumpkin
 or butternut squash
 flesh, cubed
1 tbsp hot curry paste
300 ml/½ pint

vegetable stock
1 large, firm banana
400 g can chickpeas, drained
 and rinsed
salt and freshly ground
 black pepper
1 tbsp freshly
 chopped coriander
coriander sprigs, to garnish
rice or naan bread, to serve

Heat 1 tablespoon of the oil in a saucepan and add the onion. Fry gently for 5 minutes until softened. Add the garlic, ginger and spices and fry for a further minute. Add the chopped tomatoes and chillies and cook for another minute.

Add the pumpkin and curry paste and fry gently for 3–4 minutes before adding the stock. Stir well, bring to the boil and simmer for 20 minutes until the pumpkin is tender.

Thickly slice the banana and add to the pumpkin along with the chickpeas. Simmer for a further 5 minutes.

Season to taste with salt and pepper and add the chopped coriander. Serve immediately, garnished with coriander sprigs and some rice or naan bread.

Try this: FOR AN ALTERNATIVE: 54 FOR ENTERTAINING: 52

Asian Food:
Fish & Shellfish

Prawn & Chilli Soup

2 spring onions, trimmed
225 g/8 oz whole raw
    tiger prawns
750 ml/1¼ pint fish stock
finely grated rind and

juice of 1 lime
1 tbsp fish sauce
1 red chilli, deseeded
    and chopped
1 tbsp soy sauce

1 lemon grass stalk
2 tbsp rice vinegar
4 tbsp freshly
    chopped coriander

To make spring onion curls, finely shred the spring onions lengthways. Place in a bowl of iced cold water and reserve.

Remove the heads and shells from the prawns, leaving the tails intact. Split the prawns almost in two to form a butterfly shape and individually remove the black thread that runs down the back of each one.

In a large pan heat the stock with the lime rind and juice, fish sauce, chilli and soy sauce. Bruise the lemon grass by crushing it along its length with a rolling pin, then add to the stock mixture.

When the stock mixture is boiling add the prawns and cook until they are pink. Remove the lemon grass and add the rice vinegar and coriander.

Ladle into bowls and garnish with the spring onion curls. Serve immediately.

Try this: FOR AN ALTERNATIVE: 20 FOR ENTERTAINING: 24

Crispy Prawns with Chinese Dipping Sauce

SERVES 4

450 g/1 lb medium-sized
  raw prawns, peeled
¼ tsp salt
6 tbsp groundnut oil
2 garlic cloves, peeled
  and finely chopped
2.5 cm/1 inch piece fresh root

ginger, peeled
  and finely chopped
1 green chilli, deseeded and
  finely chopped
4 stems fresh coriander,
  leaves and stems
  roughly chopped

For the Chinese dipping sauce:
3 tbsp dark soy sauce
3 tbsp rice wine vinegar
1 tbsp caster sugar
2 tbsp chilli oil
2 spring onions, finely
  shredded

Using a sharp knife, remove the black vein along the back of the prawns. Sprinkle the prawns with the salt and leave to stand for 15 minutes. Pat dry on absorbent kitchen paper.

Heat a wok or large frying pan, add the groundnut oil and when hot, add the prawns and stir-fry in 2 batches for about 1 minute, or until they turn pink and are almost cooked. Using a slotted spoon, remove the prawns and keep warm in a low oven.

Drain the oil from the wok, leaving 1 tablespoon. Add the garlic, ginger and chilli and cook for about 30 seconds. Add the coriander, return the prawns and stir-fry for 1–2 minutes, or until the prawns are cooked through and the garlic is golden. Turn into a warmed serving dish.

For the dipping sauce, using a fork, beat together the soy sauce, rice vinegar, caster sugar and chilli oil in a small bowl. Stir in the spring onions. Serve immediately with the hot prawns.

Try this: FOR AN ALTERNATIVE: 236 FOR ENTERTAINING: 250

Chilli Monkfish Stir Fry

SERVES 4

350 g/12 oz pasta twists
550 g/1¼ lb monkfish,
　　trimmed and cut
　　into chunks
2 tbsp groundnut oil
1 green chilli, deseeded
　　and cut into matchsticks

2 tbsp sesame seeds
pinch of cayenne pepper
sliced green chillies,
　　to garnish

For the marinade:
1 garlic clove, peeled

　　and chopped
2 tbsp dark soy sauce
grated zest and juice
　　of 1 lime
1 tbsp sweet chilli sauce
4 tbsp olive oil

Bring a large saucepan of lightly salted water to the boil and add the pasta. Stir, bring back to the boil and cook at a rolling boil for 8 minutes, or until 'al dente'. Drain thoroughly and reserve.

For the marinade, mix together the sliced garlic, dark soy sauce, lime zest and juice, sweet chilli sauce and olive oil in a shallow dish, then add the monkfish chunks. Stir until all the monkfish is lightly coated in the marinade, then cover and leave in the refrigerator for at least 30 minutes, spooning the marinade over the fish occasionally.

Heat a wok, then add the oil and heat until almost smoking. Remove the monkfish from the marinade, scraping off as much marinade as possible, add to the wok and stir-fry for 3 minutes. Add the green chilli and sesame seeds and stir-fry the mixture for a further 1 minute.

Stir in the pasta and marinade and stir-fry for 1–2 minutes, or until piping hot. Sprinkle with cayenne pepper and garnish with sliced green chillies. Serve immediately.

Try this: FOR AN ALTERNATIVE: 18   FOR ENTERTAINING: 230

Teriyaki Salmon

SERVES 4

450 g/1 lb salmon fillet,
  skinned
6 tbsp Japanese
  teriyaki sauce
1 tbsp rice wine vinegar
1 tbsp tomato paste

dash of Tabasco sauce
grated zest of ½ lemon
salt and freshly ground
  black pepper
4 tbsp groundnut oil
1 carrot, peeled and cut

into matchsticks
125 g/4 oz mangetout peas
125 g/4 oz oyster
  mushrooms, wiped

Using a sharp knife, cut the salmon into thick slices and place in a shallow dish. Mix together the teriyaki sauce, rice wine vinegar, tomato paste, Tabasco sauce, lemon zest and seasoning. Spoon the marinade over the salmon, then cover loosely and leave to marinate in the refrigerator for 30 minutes, turning the salmon or spooning the marinade occasionally over the salmon.

Heat a large wok, then add 2 tablespoons of the oil until almost smoking. Stir-fry the carrot for 2 minutes, then add the mangetout peas and stir-fry for a further 2 minutes. Add the oyster mushrooms and stir-fry for 4 minutes, until softened. Using a slotted spoon, transfer the vegetables to four warmed serving plates and keep warm.

Remove the salmon from the marinade, reserving both the salmon and marinade. Add the remaining oil to the wok, heat until almost smoking, then cook the salmon for 4–5 minutes, turning once during cooking, or until the fish is just flaking. Add the marinade and heat through for 1 minute. Serve immediately, with the salmon arranged on top of the vegetables and the marinade drizzled over.

Try this: FOR AN ALTERNATIVE: 302   FOR ENTERTAINING: 334

Sour & Spicy Prawn Soup

SERVES 4

50 g/2 oz rice noodles
25 g/1 oz Chinese
   dried mushrooms
4 spring onions, trimmed
2 small green chillies
3 tbsp freshly
   chopped coriander

600 ml/1 pint chicken stock
2.5 cm/1 inch piece fresh
   root ginger, peeled
   and grated
2 lemon grass stalks, outer
   leaves discarded and
   finely chopped

4 kaffir lime leaves
12 raw king prawns, peeled
   with tail shell left on
2 tbsp Thai fish sauce
2 tbsp lime juice
salt and freshly ground
   black pepper

Place the noodles in cold water and leave to soak while preparing the soup. Place the dried mushrooms in a small bowl, cover with almost boiling water and leave for 20–30 minutes. Drain, strain and reserve the soaking liquor and discard any woody stems from the mushrooms.

Finely shred the spring onions and place into a small bowl. Cover with ice cold water and refrigerate until required and the spring onions have curled.

Place the green chillies with 2 tablespoons of the chopped coriander in a pestle and mortar and pound to a paste. Reserve.

Pour the stock into a saucepan and bring gently to the boil. Stir in the ginger, lemon grass and lime leaves with the reserved mushrooms and their liquor. Return to the boil.

Drain the noodles and add to the soup with the prawns, Thai fish sauce and lime juice and then stir in the chilli and coriander paste. Bring to the boil, then simmer for 3 minutes. Stir in the remaining chopped coriander and season to taste with salt and pepper. Ladle into warmed bowls, sprinkle with the spring onions curls and serve immediately.

Try this: FOR AN ALTERNATIVE: 238   FOR ENTERTAINING: 248

Thai Crab Cakes

SERVES 4

200 g/7 oz easy-cook
  basmati rice
450 ml/¾ pint chicken
  stock, heated
200 g/7 oz cooked crab meat
125 g/4 oz cod fillet, skinned
  and minced
5 spring onions, trimmed
  and finely chopped

1 lemon grass stalk, outer
  leaves discarded and
  finely chopped
1 green chilli, deseeded
  and finely chopped
1 tbsp freshly grated
  root ginger
1 tbsp freshly
  chopped coriander

1 tbsp plain flour
1 medium egg
salt and freshly ground
  black pepper
2 tbsp vegetable oil, for frying

To serve:
sweet chilli dipping sauce
fresh salad leaves

Put the rice in a large saucepan and add the hot stock. Bring to the boil, cover and simmer over a low heat, without stirring, for 18 minutes, or until the grains are tender and all the liquid is absorbed.

To make the cakes, place the crab meat, fish, spring onions, lemon grass, chilli, ginger, coriander, flour and egg in a food processor. Blend until all the ingredients are mixed thoroughly, then season to taste with salt and pepper. Add the rice to the processor and blend once more, but do not over mix.

Remove the mixture from the processor and place on a clean work surface. With damp hands, divide into 12 even-sized patties. Transfer to a plate, cover and chill in the refrigerator for about 30 minutes.

Heat the oil in a heavy-based frying pan and cook the crab cakes, four at a time, for 3–5 minutes on each side until crisp and golden. Drain on absorbent kitchen paper and serve immediately with a chilli dipping sauce.

Try this: FOR AN ALTERNATIVE: 240 FOR ENTERTAINING: 190

Sesame Prawn Toasts

SERVES 4

125 g/4 oz peeled
   cooked prawns
1 tbsp cornflour
2 spring onions, peeled and
   roughly chopped
2 tsp freshly grated

root ginger
2 tsp dark soy sauce
pinch of Chinese five spice
   powder (optional)
1 small egg, beaten
salt and freshly ground

black pepper
6 thin slices day-old
   white bread
40 g/1½ oz sesame seeds
vegetable oil for deep-frying
chilli sauce, to serve

Place the prawns in a food processor or blender with the cornflour, spring onions, ginger, soy sauce and Chinese five spice powder, if using. Blend to a fairly smooth paste. Spoon into a bowl and stir in the beaten egg. Season to taste with salt and pepper.

Cut the crusts off the bread. Spread the prawn paste in an even layer on one side of each slice. Sprinkle over the sesame seeds and press down lightly. Cut each slice diagonally into four triangles. Place on a board and chill in the refrigerator for 30 minutes.

Pour sufficient oil into a heavy-based saucepan or deep-fat fryer so that it is one third full. Heat until it reaches a temperature of 180°C/350°F. Cook the toasts in batches of five or six, carefully lowering them seeded-side down into the oil. Deep-fry for 2–3 minutes, or until lightly browned, then turn over and cook for 1 minute more.

Using a slotted spoon, lift out the toasts and drain on absorbent kitchen paper. Keep warm while frying the remaining toasts. Arrange on a warmed platter and serve immediately with some chilli sauce for dipping.

Try this: FOR AN ALTERNATIVE: 190   FOR ENTERTAINING: 378

Thai Hot & Sour Prawn Soup

SERVES 6

700 g/1½ lb large raw prawns
2 tbsp vegetable oil
3–4 stalks lemon grass,
    outer leaves discarded
    and coarsely chopped
2.5 cm/1 inch piece fresh
    root ginger, peeled and
    finely chopped
2–3 garlic cloves,
    peeled and crushed

small bunch fresh coriander,
    leaves stripped and
    reserved, stems
    finely chopped
½ tsp freshly ground
    black pepper
1.8 litres/3¼ pints water
1–2 small red chillies,
    deseeded and
    thinly sliced

1–2 small green chillies,
    deseeded and
    thinly sliced
6 kaffir lime leaves, thinly
    shredded
4 spring onions, trimmed
    and diagonally sliced
1–2 tbsp Thai fish sauce
1–2 tbsp freshly squeezed
    lime juice

Remove the heads from the prawns by twisting away from the body and reserve. Peel the prawns, leaving the tails on and reserve the shells with the heads. Using a sharp knife, remove the black vein from the back of the prawns. Rinse and dry the prawns and reserve. Rinse and dry the heads and shells.

Heat a wok, add the oil and, when hot, add the prawn heads and shells, the lemon grass, ginger, garlic, coriander stems and black pepper and stir-fry for 2–3 minutes, or until the prawn heads and shells turn pink and all the ingredients are coloured. Carefully add the water to the wok and return to the boil, skimming off any scum which rises to the surface. Simmer over a medium heat for 10 minutes or until slightly reduced. Strain through a fine sieve and return the clear prawn stock to the wok.

Bring the stock back to the boil and add the reserved prawns, chillies, lime leaves and spring onions and simmer for 3 minutes, or until the prawns turn pink. Season with the fish sauce and lime juice. Spoon into heated soup bowls, dividing the prawns evenly and float a few coriander leaves over the surface.

Try this: FOR AN ALTERNATIVE: 182   FOR ENTERTAINING: 184

Honey & Ginger Prawns

SERVES 4

1 carrot
50 g/2 oz bamboo shoots
4 spring onions
1 tbsp clear honey
1 tbsp tomato ketchup
1 tsp soy sauce
2.5 cm/1 inch piece fresh
root ginger, peeled and

finely grated
1 garlic clove, peeled
and crushed
1 tbsp lime juice
175 g/6 oz peeled prawns,
thawed if frozen
2 heads little gem
lettuce leaves

2 tbsp freshly
chopped coriander
salt and freshly ground
black pepper

To garnish:
fresh coriander sprigs
lime slices

Cut the carrot into matchstick-sized pieces, roughly chop the bamboo shoots and finely slice the spring onions. Combine the bamboo shoots with the carrot matchsticks and spring onions.

In a wok or large frying pan gently heat the honey, tomato ketchup, soy sauce, ginger, garlic and lime juice with 3 tablespoons of water. Bring to the boil.

Add the carrot mixture and stir-fry for 2–3 minutes until the vegetables are hot. Add the prawns and continue to stir-fry for 2 minutes. Remove the wok or frying pan from the heat and reserve until cooled slightly.

Divide the little gem lettuce into leaves and rinse lightly. Stir the chopped coriander into the prawn mixture and season to taste with salt and pepper.

Spoon into the lettuce leaves and serve immediately garnished with sprigs of fresh coriander and lime slices.

Try this: FOR AN ALTERNATIVE: 80   FOR ENTERTAINING: 106

Rice with Smoked Salmon & Ginger

SERVES 4

225 g/8 oz basmati rice
600 ml/1 pint fish stock
1 bunch spring onions,
   trimmed and
   diagonally sliced
3 tbsp freshly

   chopped coriander
1 tsp grated fresh root ginger
200 g/7 oz sliced
   smoked salmon
2 tbsp soy sauce
1 tsp sesame oil

2 tsp lemon juice
4–6 slices pickled ginger
2 tsp sesame seeds
rocket leaves,
   to serve

Place the rice in a sieve and rinse under cold water until the water runs clear. Drain, then place in a large saucepan with the stock and bring gently to the boil. Reduce to a simmer and cover with a tight-fitting lid. Cook for 10 minutes, then remove from the heat and leave, covered, for a further 10 minutes.

Stir the spring onions, coriander and fresh ginger into the cooked rice and mix well. Spoon the rice into four tartlet tins, each measuring 10 cm/4 inches, and press down firmly with the back of a spoon to form cakes. Invert a tin onto an individual serving plate, then tap the base firmly and remove the tin. Repeat with the rest of the filled tins.

Top the rice with the salmon, folding if necessary, so the sides of the rice can still be seen in places. Mix together the soy sauce, sesame oil and lemon juice to make a dressing, then drizzle over the salmon.

Top with the pickled ginger and a sprinkling of sesame seeds. Scatter the rocket leaves around the edge of the plates and serve immediately.

Try this: FOR AN ALTERNATIVE: 96 FOR ENTERTAINING: 74

Thai Shellfish Soup

SERVES 4-6

350 g/12 oz raw prawns
350 g/12 oz firm white fish,
  such as monkfish,
  cod or haddock
175 g/ 6 oz small squid rings
1 tbsp lime juice

450 g/1 lb live mussels
400 ml/15 fl oz coconut milk
1 tbsp groundnut oil
2 tbsp Thai red curry paste
1 lemon grass stalk, bruised
3 kaffir lime leaves,

  finely shredded
2 tbsp Thai fish sauce
salt and freshly ground
  black pepper
fresh coriander leaves,
  to garnish

Peel the prawns. Using a sharp knife, remove the black vein along the back of the prawns. Pat dry with absorbent kitchen paper and reserve. Skin the fish, pat dry and cut into 2.5 cm/ 1 inch chunks. Place in a bowl with the prawns and the squid rings. Sprinkle with the lime juice and reserve.

Scrub the mussels, removing their beards and any barnacles. Discard any mussels that are open, damaged or that do not close when tapped. Place in a large saucepan and add 150 ml/¼ pint of coconut milk. Cover, bring to the boil, then simmer for 5 minutes, or until the mussels open, shaking the saucepan occasionally. Lift out the mussels, discarding any unopened ones, strain the liquid through a muslin-lined sieve and reserve.

Rinse and dry the saucepan. Heat the groundnut oil, add the curry paste and cook for 1 minute, stirring all the time. Add the lemon grass, lime leaves, fish sauce and pour in both the strained and the remaining coconut milk. Bring the contents of the saucepan to a very gentle simmer.

Add the fish mixture to the saucepan and simmer for 2–3 minutes or until just cooked. Stir in the mussels, with or without their shells as preferred. Season to taste with salt and pepper, then garnish with coriander leaves. Ladle into warmed bowls and serve immediately.

Try this: FOR AN ALTERNATIVE: 82   FOR ENTERTAINING: 150

Thai Fish Cakes

SERVES 4

1 red chilli, deseeded and roughly chopped
4 tbsp roughly chopped fresh coriander
1 garlic clove, peeled and crushed
2 spring onions, trimmed and roughly chopped
1 lemon grass, outer leaves discarded and roughly chopped
75 g/3 oz prawns, thawed if frozen
275 g/10 oz cod fillet, skinned, pin bones removed and cubed
salt and freshly ground black pepper
sweet chilli dipping sauce, to serve

Preheat the oven to 190°C/375°F/Gas Mark 5. Place the chilli, coriander, garlic, spring onions and lemon grass in a food processor and blend together.

Pat the prawns and cod dry with kitchen paper. Add to the food processor and blend until the mixture is roughly chopped. Season to taste with salt and pepper and blend to mix.

Dampen your hands, then shape heaped tablespoons of the mixture into 12 little patties. Place the patties on a lightly oiled baking sheet and cook in the preheated oven for 12–15 minutes, or until piping hot and cooked through. Turn the patties over halfway through the cooking time.

Serve the fish cakes immediately with the sweet chilli sauce for dipping.

Try this: FOR AN ALTERNATIVE: 152   FOR ENTERTAINING: 108

Sweetcorn & Crab Soup

SERVES 4

450 g/1 lb fresh
corn-on-the-cob
1.3 litres/2¼ pints
chicken stock
2–3 spring onions, trimmed
and finely chopped
1 cm/½ inch piece fresh root
ginger, peeled and finely

chopped
1 tbsp dry sherry or
Chinese rice wine
2–3 tsp soy sauce
1 tsp soft light brown sugar
salt and freshly ground
black pepper
2 tsp cornflour

225 g/8 oz white crab meat,
fresh or canned
1 medium egg white
1 tsp sesame oil
1–2 tbsp freshly chopped
coriander

Wash the corns cobs and dry. Using a sharp knife and holding the corn cobs at an angle to the cutting board, cut down along the cobs to remove the kernels, then scrape the cobs to remove any excess milky residue. Put the kernels and the milky residue into a large wok.

Add the chicken stock to the wok and place over a high heat. Bring to the boil, stirring and pressing some of the kernels against the side of the wok to squeeze out the starch to help thicken the soup. Simmer for 15 minutes, stirring occasionally.

Add the spring onions, ginger, sherry or Chinese rice wine, soy sauce and brown sugar to the wok and season to taste with salt and pepper. Simmer for a further 5 minutes, stirring occasionally. Blend the cornflour with 1 tablespoon of cold water to form a smooth paste and whisk into the soup. Return to the boil, then simmer over medium heat until thickened.

Add the crab meat, stirring until blended. Beat the egg white with the sesame oil and stir into the soup in a slow steady stream, stirring constantly. Stir in the chopped coriander and serve immediately.

Try this: FOR AN ALTERNATIVE: 346   FOR ENTERTAINING: 156

Steamed Monkfish with Chilli & Ginger

SERVES 4

700 g/1½ lb skinless
monkfish tail
1–2 red chillies
4 cm/1½ inch piece
fresh root ginger
1 tsp sesame oil

4 spring onions, trimmed
and thinly sliced
diagonally
2 tbsp soy sauce
2 tbsp Chinese rice wine
or dry sherry

freshly steamed rice,
to serve

To garnish:
sprigs of fresh coriander
lime wedges

Place the monkfish on a chopping board. Using a sharp knife, cut down each side of the central bone and remove. Cut the fish into 2.5cm/1 inch pieces and reserve. Make a slit down the side of each chilli, remove and discard the seeds and the membrane, then slice thinly. Peel the ginger and either chop finely or grate.

Brush a large heatproof plate with the sesame oil and arrange the monkfish pieces in one layer on the plate. Sprinkle over the spring onions and pour over the soy sauce and Chinese rice wine or sherry.

Place a wire rack or inverted ramekin in a large wok. Pour in enough water to come about 2.5 cm/1 inch up the side of the wok and bring to the boil over a high heat. Fold a long piece of tinfoil lengthways to about 5–7.5 cm/2–3 inches wide and lay it over the rack or ramekin. It must extend beyond the plate edge when it is placed in the wok.

Place the plate with the monkfish on the rack or ramekin and cover tightly. Steam over a medium-low heat for 5 minutes, or until the fish is tender and opaque. Using the tinfoil as a hammock, lift out the plate. Garnish with sprigs of coriander and lime wedges and serve immediately with steamed rice.

Try this: FOR AN ALTERNATIVE: 112   FOR ENTERTAINING: 116

Szechuan Chilli Prawns

SERVES 4

450 g/1 lb raw tiger prawns
2 tbsp groundnut oil
1 onion, peeled and sliced
1 red pepper, deseeded and
   cut into strips
1 small red chilli, deseeded
   and thinly sliced
2 garlic cloves, peeled and

finely chopped
2–3 spring onions, trimmed
   and diagonally sliced
freshly cooked rice or
   noodles, to serve
sprigs of fresh coriander
   or chilli flowers,
   to garnish

For the chilli sauce:
1 tbsp cornflour
4 tbsp cold fish stock
   or water
2 tbsp soy sauce
2 tbsp sweet or hot chilli
   sauce, or to taste
2 tsp soft light brown sugar

Peel the prawns, leaving the tails attached if you like. Using a sharp knife, remove the black vein along the back of the prawns. Rinse and pat dry with absorbent kitchen paper.

Heat a wok or large frying pan, add the oil and when hot, add the onion, pepper and chilli and stir-fry for 4–5 minutes, or until the vegetables are tender but retain a bite. Stir in the garlic and cook for 30 seconds. Using a slotted spoon, transfer to a plate and reserve.

Add the prawns to the wok and stir-fry for 1–2 minutes, or until they turn pink and opaque.

Blend all the chilli sauce ingredients together in a bowl or jug, then stir into the prawns. Add the reserved vegetables and bring to the boil, stirring constantly. Cook for 1–2 minutes, or until the sauce is thickened and the prawns and vegetables are well coated.

Stir in the spring onions, tip on to a warmed platter and garnish with chilli flowers or coriander sprigs. Serve immediately with freshly cooked rice or noodles.

Try this: FOR AN ALTERNATIVE: 84 FOR ENTERTAINING: 70

Hot Prawn Noodles with Sesame Dressing

SERVES 4

600 ml/1 pint
   vegetable stock
350 g/12 oz Chinese
   egg noodles
1 tbsp sunflower oil
1 garlic clove, peeled and
   very finely chopped

1 red chilli, deseeded and
   finely chopped
3 tbsp sesame seeds
3 tbsp dark soy sauce
2 tbsp sesame oil
175 g/6 oz shelled
   cooked prawns

3 tbsp freshly
   chopped coriander
freshly ground black pepper
fresh coriander sprigs,
   to garnish

Pour the vegetable stock into a large saucepan and bring to the boil. Add the egg noodles, stir once, then cook according to the packet instructions, usually about 3 minutes.

Meanwhile, heat the sunflower oil in a small frying pan. Add the chopped garlic and chilli and cook gently for a few seconds. Add the sesame seeds and cook, stirring continuously, for 1 minute, or until golden.

Add the soy sauce, sesame oil and prawns to the frying pan. Continue cooking for a few seconds, until the mixture is just starting to bubble, then remove immediately from the heat.

Drain the noodles thoroughly and return to the pan. Add the prawns in the dressing mixture, and the chopped coriander and season to taste with black pepper. Toss gently to coat the noodles with the hot dressing.

Tip into a warmed serving bowl or spoon on to individual plates and serve immediately, garnished with sprigs of fresh coriander.

Try this: FOR AN ALTERNATIVE: 362   FOR ENTERTAINING: 220

Sweet & Sour Fish with Crispy Noodles

SERVES 4

350 g/12 oz plaice fillets, skinned
3 tbsp plain flour
pinch of Chinese five spice powder
2.5 cm/1 inch piece fresh root ginger, peeled and grated

4 spring onions, trimmed and finely sliced
3 tbsp dry sherry
1 tbsp dark soy sauce
2 tsp soft light brown sugar
1 tsp rice or sherry vinegar
1 tsp chilli sauce
salt and freshly ground

black pepper
125 g/4 oz thin, transparent rice noodles or rice sticks
oil for deep frying

To garnish:
spring onion tassels
slices of red chilli

Cut the plaice fillets into 5 cm/2 inch slices. Mix the flour with the five spice powder in a bowl. Add the fish, a few pieces at a time, and toss to coat thoroughly. Reserve.

Place the ginger, spring onions, sherry, soy sauce, sugar, vinegar and chilli sauce in a small saucepan and season lightly with salt and pepper. Heat gently until the sugar has dissolved, then bubble the sauce for 2–3 minutes.

Break the noodles into pieces about 7.5 cm/3 inches long. Heat the oil in a deep fryer to 180˚C/350˚F. Deep-fry small handfuls of noodles for about 30 seconds, until puffed up and crisp. Remove and drain on absorbent kitchen paper.

Deep-fry the plaice for 1–2 minutes, or until firm and cooked. Remove and drain on absorbent kitchen paper.

Place the cooked fish in a warmed serving bowl, drizzle over the sauce and garnish with spring onion tassels and slices of red chilli. Pile the noodles into another bowl and serve.

Try this: FOR AN ALTERNATIVE: 102   FOR ENTERTAINING: 202

Sweet & Sour Prawns with Noodles

SERVES 4

425 g can pineapple pieces
  in natural juice
1 green pepper, deseeded
  and cut into quarters
1 tbsp groundnut oil
1 onion, cut into thin wedges

3 tbsp soft brown sugar
150 ml/¼ pint chicken stock
4 tbsp wine vinegar
1 tbsp tomato purée
1 tbsp light soy sauce
1 tbsp cornflour

350 g/12 oz raw tiger
  prawns, peeled
225 g/8 oz pak choi, shredded
350 g/12 oz medium
  egg noodles
coriander leaves, to garnish

Make the sauce by draining the pineapple and reserving 2 tablespoons of the juice. Remove the membrane from the quartered peppers and cut into thin strips. Heat the oil in a saucepan. Add the onion and pepper and cook for about 4 minutes or until the onion has softened.

Add the pineapple, the sugar, stock, vinegar, tomato purée and the soy sauce. Bring the sauce to the boil and simmer for about 4 minutes. Blend the cornflour with the reserved pineapple juice and stir into the pan, stirring until thickened.

Clean the prawns if needed. Wash the pak choi thoroughly, then shred. Add the prawns and pak choi to the sauce. Simmer gently for 3 minutes or until the prawns are cooked and have turned pink.

Cook the noodles in boiling water for 4–5 minutes until just tender. Drain and arrange the noodles on a warmed plate and pour over the sweet and sour prawns. Garnish with coriander leaves and serve immediately.

Try this: FOR AN ALTERNATIVE: 214   FOR ENTERTAINING: 126

Scallops & Prawns
Braised in Lemon Grass

SERVES 4-6

450 g/1 lb large raw prawns, peeled with tails left on
350 g/12 oz scallops, with coral attached
2 red chillies, deseeded and coarsely chopped
2 garlic cloves, peeled and coarsely chopped
4 shallots, peeled
1 tbsp shrimp paste
2 tbsp freshly chopped coriander
400 ml/14 fl oz coconut milk
2–3 lemon grass stalks, outer leaves discarded and bruised
2 tbsp Thai fish sauce
1 tbsp sugar
freshly steamed basmati rice, to serve

Rinse the prawns and scallops and pat dry with absorbent kitchen paper. Using a sharp knife, remove the black vein along the back of the prawns. Reserve.

Place the chillies, garlic, shallots, shrimp paste and 1 tablespoon of the chopped coriander in a food processor. Add 1 tablespoon of the coconut milk and 2 tablespoons of water and blend to form a thick paste. Reserve the chilli paste.

Pour the remaining coconut milk with 3 tablespoons of water into a large wok or frying pan, add the lemon grass and bring to the boil. Simmer over a medium heat for 10 minutes or until reduced slightly.

Stir the chilli paste, fish sauce and sugar into the coconut milk and continue to simmer for 2 minutes, stirring occasionally. Add the prepared prawns and scallops and simmer gently, for 3 minutes, stirring occasionally, or until cooked and the prawns are pink and the scallops are opaque.

Remove the lemon grass and stir in the remaining chopped coriander. Serve immediately spooned over freshly steamed basmati rice.

Try this: FOR AN ALTERNATIVE: 22   FOR ENTERTAINING: 142

Thai Marinated Prawns

SERVES 4

700 g/1½ lb large raw
  prawns, peeled with
  tails left on
2 large eggs
salt
50 g/2 oz cornflour
vegetable oil for deep-frying
lime wedges, to garnish

For the marinade:
2 lemon grass stalks, outer
  leaves discarded and
  bruised
2 garlic cloves, peeled and
  finely chopped
2 shallots, peeled and
  finely chopped

1 red chilli, deseeded and
  chopped
grated zest and juice of
  1 small lime
400 ml/14 fl oz coconut milk

Mix all the marinade ingredients together in a bowl, pressing on the solid ingredients to release their flavours. Season to taste with salt and reserve.

Using a sharp knife, remove the black vein along the back of the prawns and pat dry with absorbent kitchen paper. Add the prawns to the marinade and stir gently until coated evenly. Leave in the marinade for at least 1 hour, stirring occasionally.

Beat the eggs in a deep bowl with a little salt. Place the cornflour in a shallow bowl. Using a slotted spoon or spatula, transfer the prawns from the marinade to the cornflour. Stir gently until the prawns are coated on all sides and shake off any excess. Holding each prawn by its tail, dip it into the beaten egg, then into the cornflour again, shaking off any excess.

Pour enough oil into a large wok to come 5 cm/2 inches up the sides and place over a high heat. Working in batches of five or six, deep-fry the prawns for 2 minutes, or until pink and crisp, turning once. Using a slotted spoon, remove and drain on absorbent kitchen paper. Keep warm. Arrange on a warmed serving plate and garnish with lime wedges. Serve immediately.

Try this: FOR AN ALTERNATIVE: 126   FOR ENTERTAINING: 134

Deep–fried Crab Wontons

MAKES 24-30

2 tbsp sesame oil
6–8 water chestnuts, rinsed,
    drained and chopped
2 spring onions, peeled and
    finely chopped
1 cm/½ inch piece
    fresh root ginger,
    peeled and grated

185 g can white crab
    meat, drained
50 ml/2 fl oz soy sauce
2 tbsp rice wine vinegar
½ tsp dried crushed chillies
2 tsp sugar
½ tsp hot pepper sauce,
    or to taste

1 tbsp freshly chopped
    coriander or dill
1 large egg yolk
1 packet wonton skins
vegetable oil for deep-frying

lime wedges, to garnish
dipping sauce, to serve

Heat a wok or large frying pan, add 1 tablespoon of the sesame oil and when hot, add the water chestnuts, spring onions and ginger and stir-fry for 1 minute. Remove from the heat and leave to cool slightly. In a bowl, mix the crab meat with the soy sauce, rice wine vinegar, crushed chillies, sugar, hot pepper sauce, chopped coriander or dill and the egg yolk. Stir in the cooled stir-fried mixture until well blended.

Lay the wonton skins on a work surface and place 1 teaspoonful of the crab mixture on the centre of each. Brush the edges of each wonton skin with a little water and fold up one corner to the opposite corner to form a triangle. Press to seal. Bring the two corners of the triangle together to meet in the centre, brush one with a little water and overlap them, pressing to seal and form a 'tortellini' shape. Place on a baking sheet and continue with the remaining triangles.

Pour enough oil into a large wok to come 5 cm/2 inches up the sides and place over a high heat. Working in batches of five or six, fry the wontons for 3 minutes, or until crisp and golden, turning once or twice. Carefully remove the wontons with a slotted spoon, drain on absorbent kitchen paper and keep warm. Place on individual warmed serving plates, garnish each dish with a lime wedge and serve immediately with the dipping sauce.

Try this: FOR AN ALTERNATIVE: 80   FOR ENTERTAINING: 186

Chinese Steamed Sea Bass with Black Beans

SERVES 4

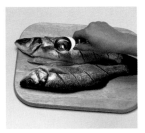

1.1 kg/2½ lb sea bass,
cleaned with head
and tail left on
1–2 tbsp rice wine or
dry sherry
1½ tbsp groundnut oil
2–3 tbsp fermented black
beans, rinsed and drained

1 garlic clove, peeled and
finely chopped
1 cm/½ inch piece fresh root
ginger, peeled and finely
chopped
4 spring onions, trimmed
and thinly sliced
diagonally

2–3 tbsp soy sauce
125 ml/4 fl oz fish or
chicken stock
1–2 tbsp sweet Chinese chilli
sauce, or to taste
2 tsp sesame oil
sprigs of fresh coriander,
to garnish

Using a sharp knife, cut 3–4 deep diagonal slashes along both sides of the fish. Sprinkle the Chinese rice wine or sherry inside and over the fish and gently rub into the skin on both sides.

Lightly brush a heatproof plate large enough to fit into a large wok or frying pan with a little of the groundnut oil. Place the fish on the plate, curving the fish along the inside edge of the dish, then leave for 20 minutes.

Place a wire rack or inverted ramekin in the wok and pour in enough water to come about 2.5 cm/1 inch up the side. Bring to the boil over a high heat. Carefully place the plate with the fish on the rack or ramekin, cover and steam for 12–15 minutes, or until the fish is tender and the flesh is opaque when pierced with a knife near the bone.

Remove the plate with the fish from the wok and keep warm. Remove the rack or ramekin from the wok and pour off the water. Return the wok to the heat, add the remaining groundnut oil and swirl to coat the bottom and side. Add the black beans, garlic and ginger and stir-fry for 1 minute. Add the spring onions, soy sauce, fish or chicken stock and boil for 1 minute. Stir in the chilli sauce and sesame oil, then pour the sauce over the cooked fish. Garnish with coriander sprigs and serve immediately.

Try this: FOR AN ALTERNATIVE: 112   FOR ENTERTAINING: 94

Steamed Whole Trout with Ginger & Spring Onion

SERVES 4

2 x 450–700 g/1–1½ lb whole
   trout, gutted with heads
   removed
coarse sea salt
2 tbsp groundnut oil
½ tbsp soy sauce
1 tbsp sesame oil
2 garlic cloves, peeled and

thinly sliced
2.5 cm/1 inch piece fresh
   root ginger, peeled and
   thinly slivered
2 spring onions, trimmed
   and thinly sliced
   diagonally

To garnish:
chive leaves
lemon slices

To serve:
freshly cooked rice
Oriental salad, to serve

Wipe the fish inside and out with absorbent kitchen paper then rub with salt inside and out and leave for about 20 minutes. Pat dry with absorbent kitchen paper.

Set a steamer rack or inverted ramekin in a large wok and pour in enough water to come about 5 cm/2 inches up the side of the wok. Bring to the boil.

Brush a heatproof dinner plate with a little of the groundnut oil and place the fish on the plate with the tails pointing in opposite directions. Place the plate on the rack, cover tightly and simmer over a medium heat for 10–12 minutes, or until tender and the flesh is opaque near the bone. Carefully transfer the plate to a heatproof surface. Sprinkle with the soy sauce and keep warm.

Pour the water out of the wok and return to the heat. Add the remaining groundnut and sesame oils and when hot, add the garlic, ginger and spring onion and stir-fry for 2 minutes, or until golden. Pour over the fish, garnish with chive leaves and lemon slices and serve immediately with rice and an Oriental salad.

Try this: FOR AN ALTERNATIVE: 110 FOR ENTERTAINING: 116

Chinese Five Spice Marinated Salmon

SERVES 4

700 g/1½ lb skinless salmon fillet, cut into 2.5 cm/ 1 inch strips
2 medium egg whites
1 tbsp cornflour
vegetable oil for frying
4 spring onions, cut diagonally into 5 cm/

2 inch pieces
125 ml/4 fl oz fish stock
lime or lemon wedges, to garnish

For the marinade:
3 tbsp soy sauce
3 tbsp Chinese rice wine or

dry sherry
2 tsp sesame oil
1 tbsp soft brown sugar
1 tbsp lime or lemon juice
1 tsp Chinese five spice powder
2–3 dashes hot pepper sauce

Combine the marinade ingredients in a shallow, non-metallic baking dish until well blended. Add the salmon strips and stir gently to coat. Leave to marinate in the refrigerator for 20–30 minutes. Using a slotted spoon or fish slice, remove the salmon pieces, drain on absorbent kitchen paper and pat dry. Reserve the marinade.

Beat the egg whites with the cornflour to make a batter. Add the salmon strips and stir into the batter until coated completely.

Pour enough oil into a large wok to come 5 cm/2 inches up the side and place over a high heat. Working in two or three batches, add the salmon strips and cook for 1–2 minutes or until golden. Remove from the wok with a slotted spoon and drain on absorbent kitchen paper. Reserve.

Discard the hot oil and wipe the wok clean. Add the marinade, spring onions and stock to the wok. Bring to the boil and simmer for 1 minute. Add the salmon strips and stir-fry gently until coated in the sauce. Spoon into a warmed shallow serving dish, garnish with the lime or lemon wedges and serve immediately.

Try this: FOR AN ALTERNATIVE: 74 FOR ENTERTAINING: 162

Fragrant Thai Swordfish with Peppers

SERVES 4-6

550 g/1¼ lb swordfish, cut into 5 cm/2 inch strips
2 tbsp vegetable oil
2 lemon grass stalks, peeled, bruised and cut into 2.5 cm/1 inch pieces
2.5 cm/1 inch piece fresh root ginger, peeled and thinly sliced
4–5 shallots, peeled and thinly sliced
2–3 garlic cloves, peeled and thinly sliced
1 small red pepper, deseeded and thinly sliced
1 small yellow pepper, deseeded and thinly sliced
2 tbsp soy sauce
2 tbsp Chinese rice wine or dry sherry
1–2 tsp sugar
1 tsp sesame oil
1 tbsp Thai or Italian basil, shredded
salt and freshly ground black pepper
1 tbsp toasted sesame seeds

For the marinade:
1 tbsp soy sauce
1 tbsp Chinese rice wine or dry sherry
1 tbsp sesame oil
1 tbsp cornflour

Blend all the marinade ingredients together in a shallow, non-metallic baking dish. Add the swordfish and spoon the marinade over the fish. Cover and leave to marinate in the refrigerator for at least 30 minutes.

Using a slotted spatula or spoon, remove the swordfish from the marinade and drain briefly on absorbent kitchen paper. Heat a wok or large frying pan, add the oil and when hot, add the swordfish and stir-fry for 2 minutes, or until it begins to brown. Remove the swordfish and drain on absorbent kitchen paper. Add the lemon grass, ginger, shallots and garlic to the wok and stir-fry for 30 seconds. Add the peppers, soy sauce, Chinese rice wine or sherry and sugar and stir-fry for 3–4 minutes.

Return the swordfish to the wok and stir-fry gently for 1–2 minutes, or until heated through and coated with the sauce. If necessary, moisten the sauce with a little of the marinade or some water. Stir in the sesame oil and the basil and season to taste with salt and pepper. Tip into a warmed serving bowl, sprinkle with sesame seeds and serve immediately.

Try this: FOR AN ALTERNATIVE: 90 FOR ENTERTAINING: 88

Spicy Cod Rice

SERVES 4

1 tbsp plain flour
1 tbsp freshly chopped coriander
1 tsp ground cumin
1 tsp ground coriander
550 g/1¼ lb thick-cut cod fillet, skinned and cut into large chunks

4 tbsp groundnut oil
50 g/2 oz cashew nuts
1 bunch spring onions, trimmed and diagonally sliced
1 red chilli, deseeded and chopped
1 carrot, peeled and cut

into matchsticks
125 g/4 oz frozen peas
450 g/1 lb cooked long-grain rice
2 tbsp sweet chilli sauce
2 tbsp soy sauce

Mix together the flour, coriander, cumin and ground coriander on a large plate. Coat the cod in the spice mixture then place on a baking sheet, cover and chill in the refrigerator for 30 minutes.

Heat a large wok, then add 2 tablespoons of the oil and heat until almost smoking. Stir-fry the cashew nuts for 1 minute, until browned, then remove and reserve.

Add a further 1 tablespoon of the oil and heat until almost smoking. Add the cod and stir-fry for 2 minutes. Using a fish slice, turn the cod pieces over and cook for a further 2 minutes, until golden. Remove from the wok, place on a warm plate, cover and keep warm.

Add the remaining oil to the wok, heat until almost smoking then stir-fry the spring onions and chilli for 1 minute before adding the carrots and peas and stir-frying for a further 2 minutes. Stir in the rice, chilli sauce, soy sauce and cashew nuts and stir-fry for 3 more minutes. Add the cod, heat for 1 minute, then serve immediately.

Try this: FOR AN ALTERNATIVE: 130   FOR ENTERTAINING: 354

Stir–fried Squid with Asparagus

SERVES 4

450 g/1 lb squid, cleaned and cut into 1 cm/ ½ inch rings
225 g/8 oz fresh asparagus, sliced diagonally into 6.5 cm/2½ inch pieces
2 tbsp groundnut oil
2 garlic cloves, peeled and

thinly sliced
2.5 cm/1 inch piece fresh root ginger, peeled and thinly sliced
225 g/8 oz pak choi, trimmed
75 ml/3 fl oz chicken stock
2 tbsp soy sauce
2 tbsp oyster sauce

1 tbsp Chinese rice wine or dry sherry
2 tsp cornflour, blended with 1 tbsp water
1 tbsp sesame oil
1 tbsp toasted sesame seeds
freshly cooked rice, to serve

Bring a medium saucepan of water to the boil over a high heat. Add the squid, return to the boil and cook for 30 seconds. Using a wide wok strainer or slotted spoon, transfer to a colander, drain and reserve. Add the asparagus pieces to the boiling water and blanch for 2 minutes. Drain and reserve.

Heat a wok or large frying pan, add the groundnut oil and when hot, add the garlic and ginger and stir-fry for 30 seconds. Add the pak choi, stir-fry for 1–2 minutes, then pour in the stock and cook for 1 minute.

Blend the soy sauce, oyster sauce and Chinese rice wine or sherry in a bowl or jug, then pour into the wok. Add the reserved squid and asparagus to the wok and stir-fry for 1 minute. Stir the blended cornflour into the wok. Stir-fry for 1 minute, or until the sauce thickens and all the ingredients are well coated.

Stir in the sesame oil, give a final stir and turn into a warmed serving dish. Sprinkle with the toasted sesame seeds and serve immediately with freshly cooked rice.

Try this: FOR AN ALTERNATIVE: 144 FOR ENTERTAINING: 140

Squid & Prawns
with Saffron Rice

SERVES 4

2 tbsp groundnut oil
1 large onion, peeled
    and sliced
2 garlic cloves, peeled
    and chopped
450 g/1 lb tomatoes,
    skinned, deseeded
    and chopped
225 g/8 oz long-grain rice

¼ tsp saffron strands
600 ml/1 pint fish stock
225 g/8 oz firm fish fillets,
    such as monkfish or cod
225 g/8 oz squid, cleaned
225 g/8 oz mussels
    with shells
75 g/3 oz frozen or shelled
    fresh peas

225 g/8 oz peeled prawns,
    thawed if frozen
salt and freshly ground
    black pepper

To garnish:
8 whole cooked prawns
lemon wedges

Heat a large wok, add the oil and when hot, stir-fry the onion and garlic for 3 minutes. Add the tomatoes and continue to stir-fry for 1 minute before adding the rice, saffron and stock. Bring to the boil, reduce the heat, cover and simmer for 10 minutes, stirring occasionally.

Meanwhile, remove any skin from the fish fillets, rinse lightly and cut into small cubes. Rinse the squid, pat dry with absorbent kitchen paper, then cut into rings and reserve. Scrub the mussels, discarding any that stay open after being tapped on the work surface. Cover with cold water and reserve until required.

Add the peas to the wok together with the fish and return to a gentle simmer. Cover and simmer for 5–10 minutes, or until the rice is tender and most of the liquid has been absorbed.

Uncover and stir in the squid, the drained prepared mussels and the peeled prawns. Re-cover and simmer for 5 minutes, or until the mussels have opened. Discard any unopened ones. Season to taste with salt and pepper. Garnish with whole cooked prawns and lemon wedges, then serve immediately.

Try this: FOR AN ALTERNATIVE: 22   FOR ENTERTAINING: 132

Scallops with Black Bean Sauce

SERVES 4

700 g/1½ lb scallops, with their coral
2 tbsp vegetable oil
2–3 tbsp Chinese fermented black beans, rinsed, drained and coarsely chopped
2 garlic cloves, peeled and finely chopped
4 cm/1½ inch piece fresh root ginger, peeled and finely chopped
4–5 spring onions, thinly sliced diagonally
2–3 tbsp soy sauce
1½ tbsp Chinese rice wine or dry sherry
1–2 tsp sugar
1 tbsp fish stock or water
2–3 dashes hot pepper sauce
1 tbsp sesame oil
freshly cooked noodles, to serve

Pat the scallops dry with absorbent kitchen paper. Carefully separate the orange coral from the scallop. Peel off and discard the membrane and thickish opaque muscle that attaches the coral to the scallop. Cut any large scallops crossways in half, leaving the corals whole.

Heat a wok or large frying pan, add the oil and when hot, add the white scallop meat and stir-fry for 2 minutes, or until just beginning to colour on the edges. Using a slotted spoon or spatula, transfer to a plate. Reserve.

Add the black beans, garlic and ginger and stir-fry for 1 minute. Add the spring onions, soy sauce, Chinese rice wine or sherry, sugar, fish stock or water, hot pepper sauce and the corals and stir until mixed.

Return the scallops and juices to the wok and stir-fry gently for 3 minutes, or until the scallops and corals are cooked through. Add a little more stock or water if necessary. Stir in the sesame oil and turn into a heated serving dish. Serve immediately with noodles.

Try this: FOR AN ALTERNATIVE: 134 FOR ENTERTAINING: 104

Stir–fried Tiger Prawns

SERVES 4

75 g/3 oz fine egg
thread noodles
125 g/4 oz broccoli florets
125 g/4 oz baby
sweetcorn, halved
3 tbsp soy sauce
1 tbsp lemon juice
pinch of sugar
1 tsp chilli sauce

1 tsp sesame oil
2 tbsp sunflower oil
450 g/1 lb raw tiger prawns,
peeled, heads and tails
removed, and de-veined
2.5 cm/1 inch piece fresh
root ginger, peeled and
cut into sticks
1 garlic clove, peeled

and chopped
1 red chilli, deseeded
and sliced
2 medium eggs,
lightly beaten
227 g can water chestnuts,
drained and sliced

Place the noodles in a large bowl, cover with plenty of boiling water and leave to stand for 5 minutes, or according to packet directions; stir occasionally. Drain and reserve. Blanch the broccoli and sweetcorn in a saucepan of boiling salted water for 2 minutes, then drain and reserve.

Meanwhile, mix together the soy sauce, lemon juice, sugar, chilli sauce and sesame oil in a bowl and reserve.

Heat a large wok, then add the sunflower oil and heat until just smoking. Add the prawns and stir-fry for 2–3 minutes, or until pink on all sides. Using a slotted spoon, transfer the prawns to a plate and reserve. Add the ginger and stir-fry for 30 seconds. Add the garlic and chilli to the wok and cook for a further 30 seconds.

Add the noodles and stir-fry for 3 minutes, until the noodles are crisp. Stir in the prawns, vegetables, eggs and water chestnuts and stir-fry for a further 3 minutes, until the eggs are lightly cooked. Pour over the chilli sauce, stir lightly and serve immediately.

Try this: FOR AN ALTERNATIVE: 136   FOR ENTERTAINING: 24

Coconut Seafood

SERVES 4

2 tbsp groundnut oil
450 g/1 lb raw king
   prawns, peeled
2 bunches spring
   onions, trimmed and
   thickly sliced
1 garlic clove, peeled
   and chopped

2.5 cm/1 inch piece fresh
   root ginger, peeled and
   cut into matchsticks
125 g/4 oz fresh shiitake
   mushrooms, rinsed
   and halved
150 ml/¼ pint dry
   white wine

200 ml/7 fl oz carton
   coconut cream
4 tbsp freshly chopped
   coriander
salt and freshly ground
   black pepper
freshly cooked fragrant
   Thai rice

Heat a large wok, add the oil and heat until it is almost smoking, swirling the oil around the wok to coat the sides. Add the prawns and stir-fry over a high heat for 4-5 minutes, or until browned on all sides. Using a slotted spoon, transfer the prawns to a plate and keep warm in a low oven.

Add the spring onions, garlic and ginger to the wok and stir-fry for 1 minute. Add the mushrooms and stir-fry for a further 3 minutes. Using a slotted spoon, transfer the mushroom mixture to a plate and keep warm in a low oven.

Add the wine and coconut cream to the wok, bring to the boil and boil rapidly for 4 minutes, until reduced slightly.

Return the mushroom mixture and prawns to the wok, bring back to the boil, then simmer for 1 minute, stirring occasionally, until piping hot. Stir in the freshly chopped coriander and season to taste with salt and pepper. Serve immediately with the freshly cooked fragrant Thai rice.

Try this: FOR AN ALTERNATIVE: 22   FOR ENTERTAINING: 18

Prawn Fried Rice

SERVES 4

knob of butter
4 medium eggs, beaten
4 tbsp groundnut oil
1 bunch spring onions,
   trimmed and finely
   shredded
125 g/4 oz cooked

ham, diced
350 g/12 oz large cooked
   prawns, thawed if frozen
   and peeled
125 g/4 oz peas,
   thawed if frozen
450 g/1 lb cooked

long-grain rice
2 tbsp dark soy sauce
1 tbsp sherry
salt and freshly ground
   black pepper
1 tbsp freshly
   shredded coriander

Heat a wok, lightly grease with the butter and when melted, pour in half the beaten eggs. Cook for 4 minutes, stirring frequently, until the egg has set, forming an omelette. Using a fish slice, lift the omelette from the wok and roll up into a sausage shape. When cool, using a sharp knife, slice the omelette into thin rings, then reserve.

Wipe the wok clean with absorbent kitchen paper and heat it. Add the oil and heat until just smoking. Add the shredded spring onions, the ham, prawns and peas and stir-fry for 2 minutes, or until heated through thoroughly. Add the cooked rice and stir-fry for a further 2 minutes.

Stir in the remaining beaten eggs and stir-fry for 3 minutes, or until the egg has set. Stir in the soy sauce and sherry and season to taste with salt and pepper, then heat until piping hot. Add the omelette rings and gently stir through the mixture, making sure not to break up the omelette rings. Sprinkle with the freshly shredded coriander and serve immediately.

Try this: FOR AN ALTERNATIVE: 262   FOR ENTERTAINING: 284

Thai Green Fragrant Mussels

SERVES 4

2 kg/4½ lb fresh mussels
4 tbsp olive oil
2 garlic cloves, peeled and
   finely sliced
3 tbsp fresh root ginger,
   peeled and finely sliced
3 lemon grass stalks, outer

leaves discarded and
   finely sliced
1–3 red or green chillies,
   deseeded and chopped
1 green pepper, deseeded
   and diced
5 spring onions, trimmed

and finely sliced
3 tbsp freshly chopped
   coriander
1 tbsp sesame oil
juice of 3 limes
400 ml can coconut milk
warm crusty bread, to serve

Scrub the mussels under cold running water, removing any barnacles and beards. Discard any that have broken or damaged shells or that are opened and do not close when tapped gently.

Heat a wok or large frying pan, add the oil and when hot, add the mussels. Shake gently and cook for 1 minute, then add the garlic, ginger, sliced lemon grass, chillies, green pepper, spring onions, 2 tablespoons of the chopped coriander and the sesame oil.

Stir-fry over a medium heat for 3–4 minutes, or until the mussels are cooked and have opened. Discard any mussels that remain unopened.

Pour the lime juice with the coconut milk into the wok and bring to the boil. Tip the mussels and the cooking liquor into warmed individual bowls. Sprinkle with the remaining chopped coriander and serve immediately with warm crusty bread.

Try this: FOR AN ALTERNATIVE: 144   FOR ENTERTAINING: 292

Oriental Spicy Scallops

SERVES 6

12 fresh scallops, trimmed
12 rashers smoked streaky
   bacon, derinded
2 tbsp groundnut oil
1 red onion, peeled and cut
   into wedges
1 red pepper, deseeded

   and sliced
1 yellow pepper, deseeded
   and sliced
2 garlic cloves, peeled and
   chopped
½ tsp garam masala
1 tbsp tomato paste

1 tbsp paprika
4 tbsp freshly
   chopped coriander

To serve:
freshly cooked noodles
Oriental-style salad

Remove the thin black thread from the scallops, rinse lightly and pat dry on absorbent kitchen paper. Wrap each scallop in a bacon rasher. Place on a baking sheet, cover and chill in the refrigerator for 30 minutes.

Meanwhile heat the wok, then add 1 tablespoon of the oil and stir-fry the onion for 3 minutes, or until almost softened. Add the peppers and stir-fry for 5 minutes, stirring occasionally, until browned. Using a slotted spoon, transfer the vegetables to a plate and reserve.

Add the remaining oil to the wok, heat until almost smoking and then add the scallops, seam-side down, and stir-fry for 2–3 minutes. Turn the scallops over and stir-fry for a further 2–3 minutes, until the bacon is crisp and the scallops are almost tender. Add the garlic, garam masala, tomato paste and paprika and stir until the scallops are lightly coated.

Stir in the remaining ingredients with the reserved vegetables. Stir-fry for a further 1–2 minutes or until the vegetables are piping hot. Serve immediately with noodles and an Oriental salad.

Try this: FOR AN ALTERNATIVE: 124   FOR ENTERTAINING: 104

Crispy Prawn Stir Fry

SERVES 4

3 tbsp soy sauce
1 tsp cornflour
pinch of sugar
6 tbsp groundnut oil
450 g/1 lb raw shelled tiger
   prawns, halved
   lengthways

125 g/4 oz carrots, peeled
   and cut into matchsticks
2.5 cm/1 inch piece fresh
   root ginger, peeled and
   cut into matchsticks
125 g/4 oz mangetout peas,
   trimmed and shredded

125 g/4 oz asparagus spears,
   cut into short lengths
125 g/4 oz beansprouts
¼ head Chinese leaves,
   shredded
2 tsp sesame oil

Mix together the soy sauce, cornflour and sugar in a small bowl and reserve.

Heat a large wok, then add 3 tablespoons of the oil and heat until almost smoking. Add the prawns and stir-fry for 4 minutes, or until pink all over. Using a slotted spoon, transfer the prawns to a plate and keep warm in a low oven.

Add the remaining oil to the wok and when just smoking, add the carrots and ginger and stir-fry for 1 minute, or until slightly softened, then add the mangetout peas and stir-fry for a further 1 minute. Add the asparagus and stir-fry for 4 minutes, or until softened.

Add the beansprouts and Chinese leaves and stir-fry for 2 minutes, or until the leaves are slightly wilted. Pour in the soy sauce mixture and return the prawns to the wok. Stir-fry over a medium heat until piping hot, then add the sesame oil, give a final stir and serve immediately.

Try this: FOR AN ALTERNATIVE: 98   FOR ENTERTAINING: 84

Fried Fish with Thai Chilli Dipping Sauce

SERVES 4

1 large egg white
½ tsp curry powder
   or turmeric
3–4 tbsp cornflour
salt and freshly ground
   black pepper
4 plaice or sole fillets, about
   225 g/8 oz each

300 ml/½ pint vegetable oil

For the dipping sauce:
2 red chillies, deseeded
   and thinly sliced
2 shallots, peeled and
   finely chopped
1 tbsp freshly squeezed

lime juice
3 tbsp Thai fish sauce
1 tbsp freshly chopped
   coriander or Thai basil

To serve:
freshly cooked rice
mixed salad leaves

To make the dipping sauce, combine all the ingredients in a bowl. Leave for at least 15 minutes. Beat the egg white until frothy and whisk into a shallow dish.

Stir the curry powder or turmeric into the cornflour in a bowl and season to taste with salt and pepper. Dip each fish fillet in the beaten egg white, dust lightly on both sides with the cornflour mixture and place on a wire rack.

Heat a wok or large frying pan, add the oil and heat to 180°C/350°F. Add one or two fillets and fry for 5 minutes, or until crisp and golden, turning once during cooking.

Using a slotted spatula, carefully remove the cooked fish and drain on absorbent kitchen paper. Keep warm while frying the remaining fillets.

Arrange the fillets on warmed individual plates and serve immediately with the dipping sauce, rice and salad.

Try this: FOR AN ALTERNATIVE: 126   FOR ENTERTAINING: 108

Warm Lobster Salad with Hot Thai Dressing

SERVES 4

1 orange
50 g/2 oz granulated sugar
2 Cos lettuce hearts, shredded
1 small avocado, peeled and
    thinly sliced
½ cucumber, peeled,
    deseeded and thinly sliced
1 ripe mango, peeled,
    stoned and thinly sliced
1 tbsp butter or vegetable oil
1 large lobster, meat
    removed and cut into

bite-sized pieces
2 tbsp Thai or Italian
    basil leaves
4 large cooked prawns,
    peeled with tails left on,
    to garnish

For the dressing:
1 tbsp vegetable oil
4–6 spring onions, trimmed
    and sliced diagonally into
    5 cm/2 inch pieces

2.5 cm/1 inch piece fresh
    root ginger, peeled
    and grated
1 garlic clove, peeled
    and crushed
grated zest of 1 lime
juice of 2–3 small limes
2 tbsp Thai fish sauce
1 tbsp brown sugar
1–2 tsp sweet chilli sauce,
    or to taste
1 tbsp sesame oil

With a sharp knife, cut the orange rind into thin julienne strips, then cook in boiling water for 2 minutes. Drain the orange strips, then plunge into cold running water, drain and return to the saucepan with the sugar and 1 cm/½ inch water. Simmer until soft, then add 1 tablespoon of cold water to stop cooking. Remove from the heat and reserve. Arrange the lettuce on four large plates and arrange the avocado, cucumber and mango slices over the lettuce.

Heat a wok or large frying pan, add the butter or oil and when hot, but not sizzling, add the lobster and stir-fry for 1–2 minutes or until heated through. Remove and drain on absorbent kitchen paper.

To make the dressing, heat the vegetable oil in a wok, then add the spring onions, ginger and garlic and stir-fry for 1 minute. Add the lime zest, lime juice, fish sauce, sugar and chilli sauce. Stir until the sugar dissolves. Remove from the heat, add the sesame oil with the orange rind and liquor. Arrange the lobster meat over the salad and drizzle with dressing. Sprinkle with basil leaves, garnish with prawns and serve immediately.

Try this: FOR AN ALTERNATIVE: 24 FOR ENTERTAINING: 142

Ginger Lobster

SERVES 4

1 celery stalk, trimmed and
    finely chopped
1 onion, peeled and
    chopped
1 small leek, trimmed
    and chopped
10 black peppercorns
1 x 550 g/1¼ lb live lobster
25 g/1 oz butter
75 g/3 oz raw prawns,

peeled and finely chopped
6 tbsp fish stock
50 g/2 oz fresh root ginger,
    peeled and cut into
    matchsticks
2 shallots, peeled and
    finely chopped
4 shiitake mushrooms,
    wiped and finely chopped
1 tsp green peppercorns,

drained and crushed
2 tbsp oyster sauce
freshly ground black pepper
¼ tsp cornflour
sprigs of fresh coriander,
    to garnish
freshly cooked Thai rice and
    mixed shredded leek,
    celery, and red chilli,
    to serve

Place the celery, onion and leek in a large saucepan with the black peppercorns. Pour in 2 litres/3½ pints of hot water, bring to the boil and boil for 5 minutes, then immerse the lobster and boil for a further 8 minutes.

Remove the lobster. When cool enough to handle, sit it on its back. Using a sharp knife, halve the lobster neatly along its entire length. Remove and discard the intestinal vein from the tail, the stomach, (which lies near the head) and the inedible gills or dead man's fingers. Remove the meat from the shell and claws and cut into pieces.

Heat a wok or large frying pan, add the butter and when melted, add the raw prawns and fish stock. Stir-fry for 3 minutes or until the prawns change colour. Add the ginger, shallots, mushrooms, green peppercorns and oyster sauce. Season to taste with black pepper. Stir in the lobster. Stir-fry for 2–3 minutes. Blend the cornflour with 1 teaspoon of water to form a thick paste, stir into the wok and cook, stirring, until the sauce thickens. Place the lobster on a warmed serving platter and tip the sauce over. Garnish and serve immediately.

Creamy Spicy Shellfish

SERVES 4

2 tbsp groundnut oil
1 onion, peeled and chopped
2.5 cm/1 inch piece fresh
   root ginger, peeled
   and grated
225 g/8 oz queen scallops,
   cleaned and rinsed
1 garlic clove, peeled

   and chopped
2 tsp ground cumin
1 tsp paprika
1 tsp coriander seeds,
   crushed
3 tbsp lemon juice
2 tbsp sherry
300 ml/½ pint fish stock

150 ml/¼ pint double cream
225 g/8 oz peeled prawns
225 g/8 oz cooked mussels,
   shelled
salt and freshly ground
   black pepper
2 tbsp freshly chopped
   coriander

Heat a large wok, then add the oil and when hot, stir-fry the onion and ginger for 2 minutes, or until softened. Add the scallops and stir-fry for 2 minutes, or until the scallops are just cooked. Using a slotted spoon, carefully transfer the scallops to a bowl and keep warm in a low oven.

Stir in the garlic, ground cumin, paprika and crushed coriander seeds and cook for 1 minute, stirring constantly. Pour in the lemon juice, sherry and fish stock and bring to the boil. Boil rapidly until reduced by half and slightly thickened.

Stir in the cream and return the scallops and any scallop juices to the wok. Bring to the boil and simmer for 1 minute. Add the prawns and mussels and heat through until piping hot. Season to taste with salt and pepper. Sprinkle with freshly chopped coriander and serve immediately.

Try this: FOR AN ALTERNATIVE: 22   FOR ENTERTAINING: 252

Tempura

SERVES 4

For the batter:
200 g/7 oz plain flour
pinch of bicarbonate of soda
1 medium egg yolk

For the prawns & vegetables:
8–12 raw king size prawns

1 carrot, peeled
125 g/4 oz button
   mushrooms, wiped
1 green pepper, deseeded
1 small aubergine, trimmed
1 onion, peeled
125 g/4 oz French beans

125 ml/4 fl oz sesame oil
300 ml/½ pint vegetable oil
   for deep frying

To serve:
soy sauce
chilli dipping sauce

Sift the flour and bicarbonate of soda into a mixing bowl. Blend 450 ml/¾ pint water and the egg yolk together, then gradually whisk into the flour mixture until a smooth batter is formed.

Peel the prawns, leaving the tails intact, de-vein, then rinse lightly and pat dry with absorbent kitchen paper and reserve. Slice the carrot thinly then, using small pastry cutters, cut out fancy shapes. Cut the mushrooms in half, if large, and cut the pepper into chunks. Slice the aubergine, then cut into chunks, together with the onion, and finally trim the French beans.

Pour the sesame oil and the vegetable oil into a large wok and heat to 180°C/350°F, or until a small spoonful of the batter dropped into the oil sizzles and cooks on impact.

Dip the prawns and vegetables into the reserved batter (no more than eight pieces at a time) and stir until lightly coated. Cook for 3 minutes, turning occasionally during cooking, or until evenly golden. Using a slotted spoon, transfer the prawns and vegetables onto absorbent kitchen paper and drain well. Keep warm. Repeat with the remaining ingredients. Serve immediately with soy sauce and chilli dipping sauce.

Try this: FOR AN ALTERNATIVE: 80   FOR ENTERTAINING: 186

Asian Food: Meat

Beef Noodle Soup

SERVES 4

900 g/2 lb boneless shin or braising steak
1 cinnamon stick
2 star anise
2 tbsp light soy sauce
6 dried red chillies or 3 fresh, chopped in half
2 dried citrus peels, soaked and diced (optional)
1.1 litre/2 pints beef or chicken stock
350 g/12 oz egg noodles
2 spring onions, trimmed and chopped, to garnish
warm chunks of crusty farmhouse bread, to serve (optional)

Trim the meat of any fat and sinew, then cut into thin strips. Place the meat, cinnamon, star anise, soy sauce, red chillies, chopped citrus peels (if using), and stock into the wok. Bring to the boil, then reduce the heat to a simmer. Skim any fat or scum that floats to the surface. Cover the wok and simmer for about 1½ hours or until the meat is tender.

Meanwhile, bring a saucepan of lightly salted water to the boil, then add the noodles and cook in the boiling water for 3–4 minutes until tender or according to packet directions. Drain well and reserve.

When the meat is tender, add the noodles to the wok and simmer for a further 1–2 minutes until the noodles are heated through thoroughly. Ladle the soup into warm shallow soup bowls or dishes and scatter with chopped spring onions. Serve, if liked, with chunks of warm crusty bread.

Try this: FOR AN ALTERNATIVE: 182   FOR ENTERTAINING: 248

Mixed Satay Sticks

SERVES 4

12 large raw prawns
350 g/12 oz beef rump steak
1 tbsp lemon juice
1 garlic clove,
   peeled and crushed
salt
2 tsp soft dark brown sugar
1 tsp ground cumin

1 tsp ground coriander
¼ tsp ground turmeric
1 tbsp groundnut oil
fresh coriander leaves,
   to garnish

For the spicy peanut sauce:
1 shallot, peeled and very

finely chopped
1 tsp demerara sugar
50 g/2 oz creamed
   coconut, chopped
pinch of chilli powder
1 tbsp dark soy sauce
125 g/4 oz crunchy
   peanut butter

Preheat the grill on high just before required. Soak eight bamboo skewers in cold water for at least 30 minutes. Peel the prawns, leaving the tails on. Using a sharp knife, remove the black vein along the back of the prawns. Cut the beef into 1 cm/½ inch wide strips. Place the prawns and beef in separate bowls and sprinkle each with ½ tablespoon of the lemon juice. Mix together the garlic, pinch of salt, sugar, cumin, coriander, turmeric and groundnut oil to make a paste. Lightly brush over the prawns and beef. Cover and place in the refrigerator to marinate for at least 30 minutes, but for longer if possible.

Meanwhile, make the sauce. Pour 125 ml/4 fl oz of water into a small saucepan, add the shallot and sugar and heat gently until the sugar has dissolved. Stir in the creamed coconut and chilli powder. When melted, remove from the heat and stir in the peanut butter. Leave to cool slightly, then spoon into a serving dish.

Thread three prawns on to each of four skewers and divide the sliced beef between the remaining skewers. Cook the skewers under the preheated grill for 4–5 minutes, turning occasionally. The prawns should be opaque and pink and the beef browned on the outside, but still pink in the centre. Transfer to warmed individual serving plates, garnish with a few fresh coriander leaves and serve immediately with the warm peanut sauce.

Spicy Beef Pancakes

SERVES 4

50 g/2 oz plain flour
pinch of salt
½ tsp Chinese five
    spice powder
1 large egg yolk
150 ml/¼ pint milk
4 tsp sunflower oil
slices of spring onion,
    to garnish

For the spicy beef filling:
1 tbsp sesame oil
4 spring onions, sliced
1 cm/½ inch piece fresh
    root ginger, peeled
    and grated
1 garlic clove,
    peeled and crushed
300 g/11 oz sirloin steak,

trimmed and cut
    into strips
1 red chilli, deseeded and
    finely chopped
1 tsp sherry vinegar
1 tsp soft dark brown sugar
1 tbsp dark soy sauce

Sift the flour, salt and Chinese five spice powder into a bowl and make a well in the centre. Add the egg yolk and a little of the milk. Gradually beat in, drawing in the flour to make a smooth batter. Whisk in the rest of the milk. Heat 1 teaspoon of the sunflower oil in a small heavy-based frying pan. Pour in just enough batter to thinly coat the base of the pan. Cook over a medium heat for 1 minute, or until the underside of the pancake is golden brown.

Turn or toss the pancake and cook for 1 minute, or until the other side of the pancake is golden brown. Make seven more pancakes with the remaining batter. Stack them on a warmed plate as you make them, with greaseproof paper between each pancake. Cover with tinfoil and keep warm in a low oven.

To make the filling, heat a wok or large frying pan, add the sesame oil and when hot, add the spring onions, ginger and garlic and stir-fry for 1 minute. Add the beef strips, stir-fry for 3–4 minutes, then stir in the chilli, vinegar, sugar and soy sauce. Cook for 1 minute, then remove from the heat. Spoon one eighth of the filling over one half of each pancake. Fold the pancakes in half, then fold in half again. Garnish with a few slices of spring onion and serve immediately.

Vietnamese Beef & Rice Noodle Soup

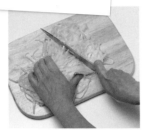

For the beef stock:
900 g/2 lb meaty beef bones
1 large onion, peeled and quartered
2 carrots, peeled and cut into chunks
2 celery stalks, trimmed and sliced
1 leek, washed and sliced into chunks

2 garlic cloves, unpeeled and lightly crushed
3 whole star anise
1 tsp black peppercorns

For the soup:
175 g/6 oz dried rice stick noodles
4–6 spring onions, trimmed and diagonally sliced

1 red chilli, deseeded and diagonally sliced
1 small bunch fresh coriander
1 small bunch fresh mint
350 g/12 oz fillet steak, very thinly sliced
salt and freshly ground black pepper

Place all the ingredients for the beef stock into a large stock pot or saucepan and cover with cold water. Bring to the boil and skim off any scum that rises to the surface. Reduce the heat and simmer gently, partially covered, for 2–3 hours, skimming occasionally.

Strain into a large bowl and leave to cool, then skim off the fat. Chill in the refrigerator and when cold remove any fat from the surface. Pour 1.7 litres/3 pints of the stock into a large wok and reserve.

Cover the noodles with warm water and leave for 3 minutes, or until just softened. Drain, then cut into 10 cm/4 inch lengths. Arrange the spring onions and chilli on a serving platter or large plate. Strip the leaves from the coriander and mint and arrange them in piles on the plate.

Bring the stock in the wok to the boil over a high heat. Add the noodles and simmer for about 2 minutes, or until tender. Add the beef strips and simmer for about 1 minute. Season to taste with salt and pepper. Ladle the soup with the noodles and beef strips into individual soup bowls and serve immediately with the plate of condiments handed around separately.

Try this: FOR AN ALTERNATIVE: 150   FOR ENTERTAINING: 346

Beef Teriyaki
with Green & Black Rice

3 tbsp sake
  (Japanese rice wine)
3 tbsp dry sherry
3 tbsp dark soy sauce
1½ tbsp soft brown sugar
4 sirloin steaks, each

weighing 175 g/6 oz,
  trimmed
350 g/12 oz long-grain and
  wild rice
2.5 cm/1 inch piece fresh
  root ginger

225 g/8 oz mangetout
salt
6 spring onions, trimmed
  and cut into fine strips

In a small saucepan, gently heat the sake, dry sherry, dark soy sauce and sugar until the sugar has dissolved. Increase the heat and bring to the boil. Remove from the heat and leave until cold. Lightly wipe the steaks, place in a shallow dish and pour the sake mixture over. Cover loosely and leave to marinate in the refrigerator for at least 1 hour, spooning the marinade over the steaks occasionally.

Cook the rice with the piece of root ginger, according to the packet instructions. Drain well, then remove and discard the piece of ginger.

Slice the mangetout thinly lengthways into fine shreds. Plunge into a saucepan of boiling salted water, return the water to the boil and drain immediately. Stir the drained mangetout and spring onions into the hot rice.

Meanwhile, heat a griddle pan until almost smoking. Remove the steaks from the marinade and cook on the hot grill pan for 3–4 minutes each side, depending on the thickness.

Place the remaining marinade in a saucepan and bring to the boil. Simmer rapidly for 2 minutes and remove from the heat. When the steaks are cooked to personal preference, leave to rest for 2–3 minutes, then slice thinly and serve with the rice and the hot marinade.

Try this: FOR AN ALTERNATIVE: 74 FOR ENTERTAINING: 180

Nasi Goreng

SERVES 4

7 large shallots, peeled
1 red chilli, deseeded and
    roughly chopped
2 garlic cloves, peeled and
    roughly chopped
4 tbsp sunflower oil
2 tsp each tomato purée and
    Indonesian sweet soy
    sauce (katjap manis)

225 g/8 oz long-grain
    white rice
125 g/4 oz French beans,
    trimmed
3 medium eggs, beaten
pinch of sugar
salt and freshly ground
    black pepper
225 g/8 oz cooked

ham, shredded
225 g/8 oz cooked peeled
    prawns, thawed if frozen
6 spring onions, trimmed
    and thinly sliced
1 tbsp light soy sauce
3 tbsp freshly
    chopped coriander

Roughly chop 1 of the shallots and place with the red chilli, garlic, 1 tablespoon of the oil, tomato purée and sweet soy sauce in a food processor and blend until smooth, then reserve. Boil the rice in plenty of salted water for 6–7 minutes until tender, adding the French beans after 4 minutes. Drain well and leave to cool. Beat the eggs with the sugar and a little salt and pepper. Heat a little of the oil in a small non-stick frying pan and add about one-third of the egg mixture. Swirl to coat the base of the pan thinly and cook for about 1 minute until golden. Flip and cook the other side briefly before removing from the pan. Roll the omelette and slice thinly into strips. Repeat with the remaining egg to make three omelettes.

Thinly slice the remaining shallots then heat a further 2 tablespoons of the oil in a clean frying pan. Add the shallots to the pan and cook for 8–10 minutes over a medium heat until golden and crisp. Drain on absorbent kitchen paper and reserve. Add the remaining 1 tablespoon of oil to a large wok or frying pan and fry the chilli paste over a medium heat for 1 minute. Add the cooked rice and beans and stir-fry for 2 minutes. Add the ham and prawns and continue stir-frying for a further 1–2 minutes. Add the omelette slices, half the fried shallots, the spring onions, soy sauce and chopped coriander. Stir-fry for a further minute until heated through. Spoon onto serving plates and garnish with the remaining crispy shallots. Serve immediately.

Try this: FOR AN ALTERNATIVE: 130   FOR ENTERTAINING: 262

Chinese Beef
with Angel Hair Pasta

SERVES 4

1 tbsp pink peppercorns
1 tbsp chilli powder
1 tbsp Szechuan pepper
3 tbsp light soy sauce
3 tbsp dry sherry
450 g/1 lb sirloin steak,
   cut into strips

350 g/12 oz angel hair pasta
1 tbsp sesame oil
1 tbsp sunflower oil
1 bunch spring onions,
   trimmed and finely
   shredded, plus extra
   to garnish

1 red pepper, deseeded and
   thinly sliced
1 green pepper, deseeded
   and thinly sliced
1 tbsp toasted sesame
   seeds, to garnish

Crush the peppercorns, using a pestle and mortar. Transfer to a shallow bowl and combine with the chilli powder, Szechuan pepper, light soy sauce and sherry. Add the beef strips and stir until lightly coated. Cover and place in the refrigerator to marinate for 3 hours; stir occasionally during this time.

When ready to cook, bring a large pan of lightly salted water to a rolling boil. Add the pasta and cook according to the packet instructions, or until 'al dente'. Drain thoroughly and return to the pan. Add the sesame oil and toss lightly. Keep the pasta warm.

Heat a wok or large frying pan, add the sunflower oil and heat until very hot. Add the shredded spring onions with the sliced red and green peppers and stir-fry for 2 minutes.

Drain the beef, reserving the marinade, then add the beef to the wok or pan and stir-fry for 3 minutes. Pour the marinade and stir-fry for 1-2 minutes, until the steak is tender.

Pile the pasta on to four warmed plates. Top with the stir-fried beef and peppers and garnish with toasted sesame seeds and shredded spring onions. Serve immediately.

Try this: FOR AN ALTERNATIVE: 170   FOR ENTERTAINING: 156

Coconut Beef

SERVES 4

450 g/1 lb beef rump or
    sirloin steak
4 tbsp groundnut oil
2 bunches spring onions,
    trimmed and thickly sliced
1 red chilli, deseeded
    and chopped

1 garlic clove, peeled and
    chopped
2 cm/1 inch piece fresh root
    ginger, peeled and cut
    into matchsticks
125 g/4 oz shiitake
    mushrooms

200 ml/7 fl oz coconut cream
150 ml/¼ pint chicken stock
4 tbsp freshly
    chopped coriander
salt and freshly ground
    black pepper
freshly cooked rice, to serve

Trim off any fat or gristle from the beef and cut into thin strips. Heat a wok or large frying pan, add 2 tablespoons of the oil and heat until just smoking. Add the beef and cook for 5–8 minutes, turning occasionally, until browned on all sides. Using a slotted spoon, transfer the beef to a plate and keep warm.

Add the remaining oil to the wok and heat until almost smoking. Add the spring onions, chilli, garlic and ginger and cook for 1 minute, stirring occasionally. Add the mushrooms and stir-fry for 3 minutes. Using a slotted spoon, transfer the mushroom mixture to a plate and keep warm.

Return the beef to the wok, pour in the coconut cream and stock. Bring to the boil and simmer for 3–4 minutes, or until the juices are slightly reduced and the beef is just tender.

Return the mushroom mixture to the wok and heat through. Stir in the chopped coriander and season to taste with salt and pepper. Serve immediately with freshly cooked rice.

Try this: FOR AN ALTERNATIVE: 128   FOR ENTERTAINING: 292

Chilli Beef

SERVES 4

550 g/1¼ lb beef
  rump steak
2 tbsp groundnut oil
2 carrots, peeled and cut
  into matchsticks
125 g/4 oz mangetout,

shredded
125 g/4 oz beansprouts
1 green chilli, deseeded
  and chopped
2 tbsp sesame seeds
freshly cooked rice, to serve

For the marinade:
1 garlic clove, peeled
  and chopped
3 tbsp soy sauce
1 tbsp sweet chilli sauce
4 tbsp groundnut oil

Using a sharp knife, trim the beef, discarding any fat or gristle, then cut into thin strips and place in a shallow dish. Combine all the marinade ingredients in a bowl and pour over the beef. Turn the beef in the marinade until coated evenly, cover with clingfilm and leave to marinate in the refrigerator for at least 30 minutes.

Heat a wok or large frying pan, add the groundnut oil and heat until almost smoking, then add the carrots and stir-fry for 3–4 minutes, or until softened. Add the mangetout and stir-fry for a further 1 minute. Using a slotted spoon, transfer the vegetables to a plate and keep warm.

Lift the beef strips from the marinade, shaking to remove excess marinade. Reserve the marinade. Add the beef to the wok and stir-fry for 3 minutes or until browned all over.

Return the stir-fried vegetables to the wok together with the beansprouts, chilli and sesame seeds and cook for 1 minute. Stir in the reserved marinade and stir-fry for 1–2 minutes or until heated through. Tip into a warmed serving dish or spoon on to individual plates and serve immediately with freshly cooked rice.

Try this: FOR AN ALTERNATIVE: 176 FOR ENTERTAINING: 230

Beef & Baby Corn Stir Fry

SERVES 4

3 tbsp light soy sauce
1 tbsp clear honey, warmed
450 g/1 lb beef rump steak, trimmed and thinly sliced
6 tbsp groundnut oil
125 g/4 oz shiitake mushrooms, wiped and halved
125 g/4 oz beansprouts, rinsed

2.5 cm/1 inch piece fresh root ginger, peeled and cut into matchsticks
125 g/4 oz mangetout, halved lengthways
125 g/4 oz broccoli, trimmed and cut into florets
1 medium carrot, peeled and cut into matchsticks
125 g/4 oz baby sweetcorn

cobs, halved lengthways
¼ head Chinese leaves, shredded
1 tbsp chilli sauce
3 tbsp black bean sauce
1 tbsp dry sherry
freshly cooked noodles, to serve

Mix together the soy sauce and honey in a shallow dish. Add the sliced beef and turn to coat evenly. Cover with clingfilm and leave to marinate for at least 30 minutes, turning occasionally.

Heat a wok or large frying pan, add 2 tablespoons of the oil and heat until just smoking. Add the mushrooms and stir-fry for 1 minute. Add the bean sprouts and stir-fry for 1 minute. Using a slotted spoon, transfer the mushroom mixture to a plate and keep warm.

Drain the beef, reserving the marinade. Reheat the wok, pour in 2 tablespoons of the oil and heat until smoking. Add the beef and stir-fry for 4 minutes or until browned. Transfer to a plate and keep warm.

Add the remaining oil to the wok and heat until just smoking. Add the ginger, mangetout, broccoli, carrot and the baby sweetcorn with the shredded Chinese leaves and stir-fry for 3 minutes. Stir in the chilli and black bean sauces, the sherry, the reserved marinade and the beef and mushroom mixture. Stir-fry for 2 minutes, then serve immediately with freshly cooked noodles.

Try this: FOR AN ALTERNATIVE: 204   FOR ENTERTAINING: 226

Szechuan Beef

SERVES 4

450 g/1 lb beef fillet
3 tbsp hoisin sauce
2 tbsp yellow bean sauce
2 tbsp dry sherry
1 tbsp brandy
2 tbsp groundnut oil
2 red chillies, deseeded
and sliced
8 bunches spring onions,
trimmed and chopped

2 garlic cloves, peeled and
chopped
2.5 cm/1 inch piece fresh
root ginger, peeled and
cut into matchsticks
1 carrot, peeled, sliced
lengthways and cut into
short lengths
2 green peppers, deseeded
and cut into 2.5 cm/1

inch pieces
227 g can water chestnuts,
drained and halved
sprigs of fresh coriander,
to garnish
freshly cooked noodles with
freshly ground Szechuan
peppercorns, to serve

Trim the beef, discarding any sinew or fat, then cut into 5 mm/¼ inch strips. Place in a large shallow dish. In a bowl, stir the hoisin sauce, yellow bean sauce, sherry and brandy together until well blended. Pour over the beef and turn until coated evenly. Cover with clingfilm and leave to marinate for at least 30 minutes.

Heat a wok or large frying pan, add the oil and when hot, add the chillies, spring onions, garlic and ginger and stir-fry for 2 minutes or until softened. Using a slotted spoon, transfer to a plate and keep warm. Add the carrot and peppers to the wok and stir-fry for 4 minutes or until slightly softened. Transfer to a plate and keep warm.

Drain the beef, reserving the marinade, add to the wok and stir-fry for 3–5 minutes or until browned. Return the chilli mixture, the carrot and pepper mixture and the marinade to the wok, add the water chestnuts and stir-fry for 2 minutes or until heated through. Garnish with sprigs of coriander and serve immediately with the noodles.

Try this: FOR AN ALTERNATIVE: 216 FOR ENTERTAINING: 310

Beef with Paprika

SERVES 4

700 g/1½ lb rump steak	long-grain rice	mushrooms,
3 tbsp plain flour	75 g/3 oz butter	wiped and sliced
salt and freshly ground	1 tsp oil	2 tsp dry sherry
black pepper	1 onion, peeled and thinly	150 ml/¼ pint soured cream
1 tbsp paprika	sliced into rings	2 tbsp freshly snipped chives
350 g/12 oz	225 g/8 oz button	bundle of chives, to garnish

Beat the steak until very thin, then trim off and discard the fat and cut into thin strips. Season the flour with the salt, pepper and paprika, then toss the steak in the flour until coated.

Meanwhile, place the rice in a saucepan of boiling salted water and simmer for 15 minutes until tender or according to packet directions. Drain the rice, then return to the saucepan, add 25 g/1 oz of the butter, cover and keep warm.

Heat the wok, then add the oil and 25 g/1 oz of the butter. When hot, stir-fry the meat for 3–5 minutes until sealed. Remove from the wok with a slotted spoon and reserve. Add the remaining butter to the wok and stir-fry the onion rings and button mushrooms for 3–4 minutes.

Add the sherry while the wok is very hot, then turn down the heat. Return the steak to the wok with the soured cream and seasoning to taste. Heat through until piping hot, then sprinkle with the snipped chives. Garnish with bundles of chives and serve immediately with the cooked rice.

Try this: FOR AN ALTERNATIVE: 164 FOR ENTERTAINING: 176

Shredded Beef in Hoisin Sauce

SERVES 4

2 celery sticks
125 g/4 oz carrots
450 g/1 lb rump steak
2 tbsp cornflour
salt and freshly ground
    black pepper

2 tbsp sunflower oil
4 spring onions, trimmed
    and chopped
2 tbsp light soy sauce
1 tbsp hoisin sauce
1 tbsp sweet chilli sauce

2 tbsp dry sherry
250 g pack fine egg
    thread noodles
1 tbsp freshly
    chopped
coriander

Trim the celery and peel the carrots, then cut into fine matchsticks and reserve.

Place the steak between two sheets of greaseproof paper or baking parchment. Beat the steak with a meat mallet or rolling pin until very thin, then slice into strips. Season the cornflour with salt and pepper and use to coat the steak. Reserve.

Heat a wok, add the oil and when hot, add the spring onions and cook for 1 minute, then add the steak and stir-fry for a further 3–4 minutes, or until the meat is sealed.

Add the celery and carrot matchsticks to the wok and stir-fry for a further 2 minutes before adding the soy, hoisin and chilli sauces and the sherry. Bring to the boil and simmer for 2–3 minutes, or until the steak is tender and the vegetables are cooked.

Plunge the fine egg noodles into boiling water and leave for 4 minutes. Drain, then spoon onto a large serving dish. Top with the cooked shredded steak, then sprinkle with chopped coriander and serve immediately.

Try this: FOR AN ALTERNATIVE: 212   FOR ENTERTAINING: 282

Fried Rice with Chilli Beef

SERVES 4

225 g/8 oz beef fillet
375 g/12 oz long-grain rice
4 tbsp groundnut oil
3 onions, peeled and
   thinly sliced

2 hot red chillies, deseeded
   and finely chopped
2 tbsp light soy sauce
2 tsp tomato paste
salt and freshly ground

black pepper
2 tbsp milk
2 tbsp flour
15 g/ ½ oz butter
2 medium eggs

Trim the beef fillet, discarding any fat, then cut into thin strips and reserve. Cook the rice in boiling salted water for 15 minutes or according to packet directions, then drain and reserve.

Heat a wok and add 3 tablespoons of oil. When hot, add 2 of the sliced onions and stir-fry for 2–3 minutes. Add the beef to the wok, together with the chillies, and stir-fry for a further 3 minutes, or until tender.

Add the rice to the wok with the soy sauce and tomato paste. Stir-fry for 1–2 minutes, or until piping hot. Season to taste with salt and pepper and keep warm. Meanwhile, toss the remaining onion in the milk, then the flour in batches. In a small frying pan fry the onion in the last 1 tablespoon of oil until crisp, then reserve.

Melt the butter in a small omelette pan. Beat the eggs with 2 teaspoons of water and pour into the pan. Cook gently, stirring frequently, until the egg has set, forming an omelette, then slide onto a clean chopping board and cut into thin strips. Add to the fried rice, sprinkle with the crispy onion and serve immediately.

Try this: FOR AN ALTERNATIVE: 160   FOR ENTERTAINING: 130

Dim Sum Pork Parcels

MAKES ABOUT 40

125 g/4 oz canned water chestnuts, drained and finely chopped

125 g/4 oz raw prawns, peeled, deveined and coarsely chopped

350 g/12 oz fresh pork mince

2 tbsp smoked bacon, finely chopped

1 tbsp light soy sauce, plus extra, to serve

1 tsp dark soy sauce

1 tbsp Chinese rice wine

2 tbsp fresh root ginger, peeled and finely chopped

3 spring onions, trimmed and finely chopped

2 tsp sesame oil

1 medium egg white, lightly beaten

salt and freshly ground black pepper

2 tsp sugar

40 wonton skins, thawed if frozen

toasted sesame seeds, to garnish

soy sauce, to serve

Place the water chestnuts, prawns, pork mince and bacon in a bowl and mix together. Add the soy sauces, Chinese rice wine, ginger, chopped spring onion, sesame oil and egg white. Season to taste with salt and pepper, sprinkle in the sugar and mix the filling thoroughly.

Place a spoonful of filling in the centre of a wonton skin. Bring the sides up and press around the filling to make a basket shape. Flatten the base of the skin, so the wonton stands solid. The top should be wide open, exposing the filling.

Place the parcels on a heatproof plate, on a wire rack inside a wok or on the base of a muslin-lined bamboo steamer. Place over a wok, half-filled with boiling water, cover, then steam the parcels for about 20 minutes. Do this in two batches. Transfer to a warmed serving plate, sprinkle with toasted sesame seeds, drizzle with soy sauce and serve immediately.

Try this: FOR AN ALTERNATIVE: 186   FOR ENTERTAINING: 200

Moo Shi Pork

SERVES 4

175 g/6 oz pork fillet
2 tsp Chinese rice wine or
  dry sherry
2 tbsp light soy sauce
1 tsp cornflour
25 g/1 oz dried
  golden needles,
  soaked and drained

2 tbsp groundnut oil
3 medium eggs,
  lightly beaten
1 tsp freshly grated
  root ginger
3 spring onions, trimmed
  and thinly sliced
150 g/5 oz bamboo shoots,

cut into fine strips
salt and freshly ground
  black pepper
8 mandarin pancakes,
  steamed
hoisin sauce
sprigs of fresh coriander,
  to garnish

Cut the pork across the grain into 1 cm/½ inch slices, then cut into thin strips. Place in a bowl with the Chinese rice wine or sherry, soy sauce and cornflour. Mix well and reserve. Trim off the tough ends of the golden needles, then cut in half and reserve.

Heat a wok or large frying pan, add 1 tablespoon of the groundnut oil and when hot, add the lightly beaten eggs, and cook for 1 minute, stirring all the time, until scrambled. Remove and reserve. Wipe the wok clean with absorbent kitchen paper.

Return the wok to the heat, add the remaining oil and when hot transfer the pork strips from the marinade mixture to the wok, shaking off as much marinade as possible. Stir-fry for 30 seconds, then add the ginger, spring onions and bamboo shoots and pour in the marinade. Stir-fry for 2–3 minutes or until cooked.

Return the scrambled eggs to the wok, season to taste with salt and pepper and stir for a few seconds until mixed well and heated through. Divide the mixture between the pancakes, drizzle each with 1 teaspoon of hoisin sauce and roll up. Garnish and serve immediately.

Try this: FOR AN ALTERNATIVE: 154   FOR ENTERTAINING: 160

Chinese Leaf & Mushroom Soup

SERVES 4-6

450 g/1 lb Chinese leaves
25 g/1 oz dried Chinese
  (shiitake) mushrooms
1 tbsp vegetable oil
75 g/3 oz smoked streaky
  bacon, diced
2.5 cm/1 inch piece fresh

root ginger, peeled and
  finely chopped
175 g/6 oz chestnut
  mushrooms, thinly sliced
1.1 litres/2 pints
  chicken stock
4–6 spring onions, trimmed

and cut into short lengths
2 tbsp dry sherry or
  Chinese rice wine
salt and freshly ground
  black pepper
sesame oil for drizzling

Trim the stem ends of the Chinese leaves and cut in half lengthways. Remove the triangular core with a knife, then cut into 2.5 cm/1 inch slices and reserve. Place the dried Chinese mushrooms in a bowl and pour over enough almost boiling water to cover. Leave to stand for 20 minutes to soften, then gently lift out and squeeze out the liquid. Discard the stems and thinly slice the caps and reserve. Strain the liquid through a muslin-lined sieve or a coffee filter paper and reserve.

Heat a wok over a medium-high heat, add the oil and when hot add the bacon. Stir-fry for 3–4 minutes, or until crisp and golden, stirring frequently. Add the ginger and chestnut mushrooms and stir-fry for a further 2–3 minutes.

Add the chicken stock and bring to the boil, skimming any fat and scum that rises to the surface. Add the spring onions, sherry or rice wine, Chinese leaves, sliced Chinese mushrooms and season to taste with salt and pepper. Pour in the reserved soaking liquid and reduce the heat to the lowest possible setting.

Simmer gently, covered, until all the vegetables are very tender; this will take about 10 minutes. Add a little water if the liquid has reduced too much. Spoon into soup bowls and drizzle with a little sesame oil. Serve immediately.

Try this: FOR AN ALTERNATIVE: 150   FOR ENTERTAINING: 68

Wonton Noodle Soup

SERVES 4

4 shiitake mushrooms, wiped
125 g/4 oz raw prawns, peeled and finely chopped
125 g/4 oz pork mince
4 water chestnuts, finely chopped

4 spring onions, trimmed and finely sliced
1 medium egg white
salt and freshly ground black pepper
1½ tsp cornflour
1 packet fresh wonton

wrappers
1.1 litres/2 pints chicken stock
2 cm/¾ inch piece root ginger, peeled and sliced
75 g/3 oz thin egg noodles
125 g/4 oz pak choi, shredded

Place the mushrooms in a bowl, cover with warm water and leave to soak for 1 hour. Drain, remove and discard the stalks and finely chop the mushrooms. Return to the bowl with the prawns, pork, water chestnuts, 2 of the spring onions and egg white. Season to taste with salt and pepper. Mix well.

Mix the cornflour with 1 tablespoon of cold water to make a paste. Place a wonton wrapper on a board and brush the edges with the paste. Drop a little less than 1 teaspoon of the pork mixture in the centre then fold in half to make a triangle, pressing the edges together. Bring the two outer corners together, fixing together with a little more paste. Continue until all the pork mixture is used up; you should have 16–20 wontons.

Pour the stock into a large wide saucepan, add the ginger slices and bring to the boil. Add the wontons and simmer for about 5 minutes. Add the noodles and cook for 1 minute. Stir in the pak choi and cook for a further 2 minutes, or until the noodles and pak choi are tender and the wontons have floated to the surface and are cooked through.

Ladle the soup into warmed bowls, discarding the ginger. Sprinkle with the remaining sliced spring onion and serve immediately.

Try this: FOR AN ALTERNATIVE: 186   FOR ENTERTAINING: 336

Crispy Pork Wontons

SERVES 4

1 small onion, peeled and roughly chopped
2 garlic cloves, peeled and crushed
1 green chilli, deseeded and chopped
2.5 cm/1 inch piece fresh

root ginger, peeled and roughly chopped
450 g/1 lb lean pork mince
4 tbsp freshly chopped coriander
1 tsp Chinese five spice powder

salt and freshly ground black pepper
20 wonton wrappers
1 medium egg, lightly beaten
vegetable oil for deep-frying
chilli sauce, to serve

Place the onion, garlic, chilli and ginger in a food processor and blend until very finely chopped. Add the pork, coriander and Chinese five spice powder. Season to taste with salt and pepper, then blend again briefly to mix. Divide the mixture into 20 equal portions and with floured hands shape each into a walnut-sized ball.

Brush the edges of a wonton wrapper with beaten egg, place a pork ball in the centre, then bring the corners to the centre and pinch together to make a money bag. Repeat with the remaining pork balls and wrappers.

Pour sufficient oil into a heavy-based saucepan or deep-fat fryer so that it is one third full and heat to 180°C/350°F. Deep-fry the wontons in three or four batches for 3–4 minutes, or until cooked through and golden and crisp. Drain on absorbent kitchen paper. Serve the crispy pork wontons immediately, allowing five per person, with some chilli sauce for dipping.

Try this: FOR AN ALTERNATIVE: 190   FOR ENTERTAINING: 178

Spring Rolls

MAKES 26–30 ROLLS

For the filling:
15 g/½ oz dried Chinese (shiitake) mushrooms
50 g/2 oz rice vermicelli
1–2 tbsp groundnut oil
1 small onion, peeled and finely chopped
3–4 garlic cloves, peeled and finely chopped
4 cm/1½ inch piece fresh root ginger, peeled and chopped
225 g/8 oz fresh pork mince
2 spring onions, trimmed and finely chopped
75 g/3 oz beansprouts
4 water chestnuts, chopped
2 tbsp freshly snipped chives
175 g/6 oz cooked peeled prawns, chopped
1 tsp oyster sauce
1 tsp soy sauce
salt and freshly ground black pepper
spring onion tassels, to garnish

For the wrappers:
4–5 tbsp plain flour
26–30 spring roll wrappers
300 ml/½ pint vegetable oil for deep frying

Soak the Chinese mushrooms in almost boiling water for 20 minutes. Remove and squeeze out the liquid. Discard any stems, slice and reserve. Soak the rice vermicelli as packet instructions. Heat a large wok and when hot, add the oil. Heat then add the onion, garlic and ginger and stir-fry for 2 minutes. Add the pork, spring onions and Chinese mushrooms and stir-fry for 4 minutes. Stir in the beansprouts, water chestnuts, chives, prawns, oyster and soy sauce. Season to taste with salt and pepper and spoon into a bowl. Drain the noodles well, add to the bowl and toss until well mixed, then leave to cool.

Blend the flour to a smooth paste with 3–4 tablespoons of water. Soften a wrapper in a plate of warm water for 1–2 seconds, then drain. Put 2 tablespoons of the filling near one edge of the wrapper, fold the edge over the filling, then fold in each side and roll up. Seal with a little flour paste and transfer to a baking sheet, seam-side down. Repeat with the remaining wrappers. Heat the oil in a large wok to 190°C/375°F, or until a cube of bread browns in 30 seconds. Fry the spring rolls a few at a time, until golden. Remove and drain on absorbent kitchen paper. Arrange on a serving plate and garnish with spring onion tassels. Serve immediately.

Try this: FOR AN ALTERNATIVE: 254   FOR ENTERTAINING: 278

Barbecue Pork Steamed Buns

SERVES 12

For the buns:
175–200 g/6–7 oz plain flour
1 tbsp dried yeast
125 ml/4 fl oz milk
2 tbsp sunflower oil
1 tbsp sugar
½ tsp salt
spring onion tassels,

to garnish
fresh green salad leaves,
to serve

For the filling:
2 tbsp vegetable oil
1 small red pepper, deseeded
and finely chopped

2 garlic cloves, peeled and
finely chopped
225 g/8 oz cooked pork,
finely chopped
50 g/2 oz light brown sugar
50 ml/2 fl oz tomato ketchup
1–2 tsp hot chilli powder,
or to taste

Put 75 g/3 oz of the flour in a bowl and stir in the yeast. Heat the milk, oil, sugar and salt in a small saucepan until warm, stirring until the sugar has dissolved. Pour into the bowl and, with an electric mixer, beat on a low speed for 30 seconds, scraping down the sides of the bowl, until blended. Beat at high speed for 3 minutes, then with a wooden spoon, stir in as much of the remaining flour as possible, until a stiff dough forms. Shape into a ball, place in a lightly oiled bowl, cover with clingfilm and leave for 1 hour in a warm place, or until doubled in size.

To make the filling, heat a wok, add the oil and when hot add the red pepper and garlic. Stir-fry for 4–5 minutes. Add the remaining ingredients and bring to the boil, stir-frying for 2–3 minutes until thick and syrupy. Cool and reserve. Punch down the dough and turn onto a lightly floured surface. Divide into 12 pieces and shape them into balls, then cover and leave to rest for 5 minutes. Roll each ball to a 7.5 cm/ 3 inch circle. Place a heaped tablespoon of filling in the centre of each. Dampen the edges, then bring them up and around the filling, pinching together to seal. Place seam-side down on a small square of non-stick baking parchment. Continue with the remaining dough and filling. Leave to rise for 10 minutes. Bring a large wok half-filled with water to the boil, place the buns in a lightly oiled Chinese steamer, without touching each other. Cover and steam for 20–25 minutes, then remove and cool slightly. Garnish with spring onion tassels and serve with salad leaves.

Try this: FOR AN ALTERNATIVE: 260   FOR ENTERTAINING: 348

Pork Fried Noodles

SERVES 4

125 g/4 oz dried thread
   egg noodles
125 g/4 oz broccoli florets
4 tbsp groundnut oil
350 g/12 oz pork tenderloin,
   cut into slices
3 tbsp soy sauce
1 tbsp lemon juice
pinch of sugar

1 tsp chilli sauce
1 tbsp sesame oil
2.5 cm/1 inch piece fresh
   root ginger, peeled and
   cut into sticks
1 garlic clove,
   peeled and chopped
1 green chilli,
   deseeded and sliced

125 g/4 oz mangetout, halved
2 medium eggs, lightly
   beaten
227 g can water chestnuts,
   drained and sliced

To garnish:
radish rose
spring onion tassels

Place the noodles in a bowl and cover with boiling water. Leave to stand for 20 minutes, stirring occasionally, or until tender. Drain and reserve. Meanwhile, blanch the broccoli in a saucepan of lightly salted boiling water for 2 minutes. Drain, refresh under cold running water and reserve.

Heat a large wok or frying pan, add the groundnut oil and heat until just smoking. Add the pork and stir-fry for 5 minutes, or until browned. Using a slotted spoon, remove the pork slices and reserve. Mix together the soy sauce, lemon juice, sugar, chilli sauce and sesame oil and reserve.

Add the ginger to the wok and stir-fry for 30 seconds. Add the garlic and chilli and stir-fry for 30 seconds. Add the reserved broccoli and stir-fry for 3 minutes. Stir in the mangetout, pork and reserved noodles with the beaten eggs and water chestnuts and stir-fry for 5 minutes or until heated through. Pour over the reserved chilli sauce, toss well and turn into a warmed serving dish. Garnish and serve immediately.

Try this: FOR AN ALTERNATIVE: 360   FOR ENTERTAINING: 374

Hoisin Pork

SERVES 4

1.4 kg/3 lb piece lean
   belly pork, boned
sea salt
2 tsp Chinese five

   spice powder
2 garlic cloves,
   peeled and chopped
1 tsp sesame oil

4 tbsp hoisin sauce
1 tbsp clear honey
assorted salad leaves,
   to garnish

Preheat the oven to 200°C/400°F/Gas Mark 6, 15 minutes before cooking. Using a sharp knife, cut the pork skin in a criss-cross pattern, making sure not to cut all the way through into the flesh. Rub the salt evenly over the skin and leave to stand for 30 minutes.

Meanwhile, mix together the five spice powder, garlic, sesame oil, hoisin sauce and honey until smooth. Rub the mixture evenly over the pork skin. Place the pork on a plate and chill in the refrigerator to marinate for up to 6 hours.

Place the pork on a wire rack set inside a roasting tin and roast the pork in the preheated oven for 1–1¼ hours, or until the pork is very crisp and the juices run clear when pierced with a skewer.

Remove the pork from the heat, leave to rest for 15 minutes, then cut into strips. Arrange on a warmed serving platter. Garnish with salad leaves and serve immediately.

Try this: FOR AN ALTERNATIVE: 266   FOR ENTERTAINING: 158

Pork with Tofu & Coconut

SERVES 4

50 g/2 oz unsalted
  cashew nuts
1 tbsp ground coriander
1 tbsp ground cumin
2 tsp hot chilli powder
2.5 cm/1 inch piece fresh
  root ginger, peeled
  and chopped
1 tbsp oyster sauce

4 tbsp groundnut oil
400 ml/14 fl oz coconut milk
175 g/6 oz rice noodles
450 g/1 lb pork tenderloin,
  thickly sliced
1 red chilli, deseeded
  and sliced
1 green chilli, deseeded
  and sliced

1 bunch spring onions,
  trimmed and thickly sliced
3 tomatoes, roughly chopped
75 g/3 oz tofu, drained
2 tbsp freshly chopped
  coriander
2 tbsp freshly chopped mint
salt and freshly ground
  black pepper

Place the cashew nuts, coriander, cumin, chilli powder, ginger and oyster sauce in a food processor and blend until well ground. Heat a wok or large frying pan, add 2 tablespoons of the oil and when hot, add the cashew mixture and stir-fry for 1 minute. Stir in the coconut milk, bring to the boil, then simmer for 1 minute. Pour into a small jug and reserve. Wipe the wok clean.

Meanwhile, place the rice noodles in a bowl, cover with boiling water, leave to stand for 5 minutes, then drain thoroughly.

Reheat the wok, add the remaining oil and when hot, add the pork and stir-fry for 5 minutes or until browned all over. Add the chillies and spring onions and stir-fry for 2 minutes.

Add the tomatoes and tofu to the wok with the noodles and coconut mixture and stir-fry for a further 2 minutes, or until heated through, being careful not to break up the tofu. Sprinkle with the chopped coriander and mint, season to taste with salt and pepper and stir. Tip into a warmed serving dish and serve immediately.

Try this: FOR AN ALTERNATIVE: 364   FOR ENTERTAINING: 60

Pork with Black Bean Sauce

SERVES 4

700 g/1½ lb pork tenderloin
4 tbsp light soy sauce
2 tbsp groundnut oil
1 garlic clove,
   peeled and chopped
2.5 cm/1 inch piece fresh
   root ginger, peeled and

cut into matchsticks
1 large carrot,
   peeled and sliced
1 red pepper,
   deseeded and sliced
1 green pepper,
   deseeded and sliced

160 g jar black bean sauce
salt
snipped fresh chives,
   to garnish
freshly steamed rice,
   to serve

Using a sharp knife, trim the pork, discarding any fat or sinew and cut into bite-sized chunks. Place in a large shallow dish and spoon over the soy sauce. Turn to coat evenly, cover with clingfilm and leave to marinate for at least 30 minutes. When in the refrigerator ready to use, lift the pork from the marinade, shaking off as much marinade as possible, and pat dry with absorbent kitchen paper. Reserve the marinade.

Heat a wok, add the groundnut oil and when hot, add the chopped garlic and ginger and stir-fry for 30 seconds. Add the carrot and the red and green peppers and stir-fry for 3–4 minutes or until just softened.

Add the pork to the wok and stir-fry for 5–7 minutes, or until browned all over and tender. Pour in the reserved marinade and black bean sauce. Bring to the boil, stirring constantly until well blended, then simmer for 1 minute, until heated through thoroughly.

Tip into a warmed serving dish or spoon on to individual plates. Garnish with snipped chives and serve immediately with steamed rice.

Try this: FOR AN ALTERNATIVE: 210   FOR ENTERTAINING: 282

Pork Spring Rolls

SERVES 4

125 g/4 oz pork tenderloin
2 tbsp light soy sauce
225 ml/8 fl oz groundnut oil
1 medium carrot, peeled and cut into matchsticks
75 g/3 oz button mushrooms, wiped and sliced
4 spring onions, trimmed and thinly sliced
75 g/3 oz beansprouts
1 garlic clove, peeled and chopped
1 tbsp dark soy sauce
12 large sheets filo pastry folded in half
spring onion curls, to garnish
Chinese-style dipping sauce, to serve

Trim the pork, discarding any sinew or fat, and cut into very fine strips. Place in a small bowl, pour over the light soy sauce and stir until well coated. Cover with clingfilm and leave to marinate in the refrigerator for at least 30 minutes.

Heat a wok or large frying pan, add 1 tablespoon of the oil and when hot, add the carrot and mushrooms and stir-fry for 3 minutes or until softened. Add the spring onions, beansprouts and garlic, stir-fry for 2 minutes, then transfer the vegetables to a bowl and reserve.

Drain the pork well, add to the wok and stir-fry for 2–4 minutes or until browned. Add the pork to the vegetables and leave to cool. Stir in the dark soy sauce and mix the filling well.

Lay the folded filo pastry sheets on a work surface. Divide the filling between the sheets, placing it at one end. Brush the filo edges with water, then fold the sides over and roll up.

Heat the remaining oil in a large wok to 180°C/350°F and cook the spring rolls in batches for 2–3 minutes, or until golden, turning the rolls during cooking. Using a slotted spoon, remove and drain on absorbent kitchen paper. Garnish with spring onion curls and serve immediately with a Chinese-style dipping sauce.

Try this: FOR AN ALTERNATIVE: 186   FOR ENTERTAINING: 376

Sweet & Sour Spareribs

SERVES 4

1.6 kg/3½ lb pork spareribs	4 tbsp soy sauce	1½ tbsp tomato purée
4 tbsp clear honey	2½ tbsp dry sherry	1 tsp dry mustard powder
1 tbsp Worcestershire sauce	1 tsp chilli sauce	(optional)
1 tsp Chinese five	2 garlic cloves,	spring onion curls,
spice powder	peeled and chopped	to garnish

Preheat the oven to 200°C/400°F/Gas Mark 6, 15 minutes before cooking. If necessary, place the ribs on a chopping board and using a sharp knife, cut the joint in between the ribs, to form single ribs. Place the ribs in a shallow dish in a single layer.

Spoon the honey, the Worcestershire sauce, Chinese five spice powder with the soy sauce, sherry and chilli sauce into a small saucepan and heat gently, stirring until smooth. Stir in the chopped garlic, the tomato purée and mustard powder, if using.

Pour the honey mixture over ribs and spoon over until the ribs are coated evenly. Cover with clingfilm and leave to marinate overnight in the refrigerator, occasionally spooning the marinade over the ribs.

When ready to cook, remove the ribs from the marinade and place in a shallow roasting tin. Spoon over a little of the marinade and reserve the remainder. Place the spareribs in the preheated oven and cook for 35–40 minutes, or until cooked and the outsides are crisp. Baste occasionally with the reserved marinade during cooking. Garnish with a few spring onion curls and serve immediately, either as a starter or as a meat accompaniment.

Try this: FOR AN ALTERNATIVE: 194   FOR ENTERTAINING: 278

Cashew & Pork Stir Fry

SERVES 4

450 g/1 lb pork tenderloin
4 tbsp soy sauce
1 tbsp cornflour
125 g/4 oz unsalted
  cashew nuts
4 tbsp sunflower oil
450 g/1 lb leeks, trimmed
and shredded
2.5 cm/1 inch piece fresh
  root ginger, peeled and
  cut into matchsticks
2 garlic cloves,
  peeled and chopped
1 red pepper,
deseeded and sliced
300 ml/½ pint chicken stock
2 tbsp freshly chopped
  coriander
freshly cooked noodles,
  to serve

Using a sharp knife, trim the pork, discarding any sinew or fat. Cut into 2 cm/¾ inch slices and place in a shallow dish. Blend the soy sauce and cornflour together until smooth and free from lumps, then pour over the pork. Stir until coated in the cornflour mixture, then cover with clingfilm and leave to marinate in the refrigerator for at least 30 minutes.

Heat a non-stick frying pan until hot, add the cashew nuts and dry-fry for 2–3 minutes, or until toasted, stirring frequently. Transfer to a plate and reserve.

Heat a wok or large frying pan, add 2 tablespoons of the oil and when hot, add the leeks, ginger, garlic and pepper and stir-fry for 5 minutes or until softened. Using a slotted spoon, transfer to a plate and keep warm.

Drain the pork, reserving the marinade. Add the remaining oil to the wok and when hot, add the pork and stir-fry for 5 minutes or until browned. Return the reserved vegetables to the wok with the marinade and the stock. Bring to the boil, then simmer for 2 minutes, or until the sauce has thickened. Stir in the toasted cashew nuts and chopped coriander and serve immediately with freshly cooked noodles.

Try this: FOR AN ALTERNATIVE: 168   FOR ENTERTAINING: 366

Barbecued Pork Fillet

SERVES 4

2 tbsp clear honey
2 tbsp hoisin sauce
2 tsp tomato purée
2.5 cm/1 inch piece fresh
    root ginger, peeled
    and chopped
450 g/1 lb pork tenderloin
3 tbsp vegetable oil

1 garlic clove, peeled and
    chopped
1 bunch spring onions,
    trimmed and chopped
1 red pepper, deseeded and
    cut into chunks
1 yellow pepper, deseeded
    and cut into chunks

350 g/12 oz cooked
    long-grain rice
125 g/4 oz frozen peas,
    thawed
2 tbsp light soy sauce
1 tbsp sesame oil
50 g/2 oz toasted
    flaked almonds

Preheat the oven to 200°C/400°F/Gas Mark 6, 15 minutes before cooking. Mix together the honey, hoisin sauce, tomato purée and ginger in a bowl. Trim the pork, discarding any sinew or fat. Place in a shallow dish and spread the honey and hoisin sauce over the pork to cover completely. Cover with clingfilm and chill in the refrigerator for 4 hours, turning occasionally.

Remove the pork from the marinade and place in a roasting tin, reserving the marinade. Cook in the preheated oven for 20–25 minutes, or until the pork is tender and the juices run clear when pierced with a skewer. Baste occasionally during cooking with the reserved marinade. Remove the pork from the oven, leave to rest for 5 minutes, then slice thinly and keep warm.

Meanwhile, heat a wok or large frying pan, add the vegetable oil and when hot, add the garlic, spring onions and peppers and stir-fry for 4 minutes or until softened. Add the rice and peas and stir-fry for 2 minutes.

Add the soy sauce, sesame oil and flaked almonds and stir-fry for 30 seconds or until heated through. Tip into a warmed serving dish and top with the sliced pork. Serve immediately.

Try this: FOR AN ALTERNATIVE: 202   FOR ENTERTAINING: 194

Crispy Pork with Tangy Sauce

SERVES 4

350 g/12 oz pork fillet
1 tbsp light soy sauce
1 tbsp dry sherry
salt and freshly ground
    black pepper
1 tbsp sherry vinegar

1 tbsp tomato paste
1 tbsp dark soy sauce
2 tsp light muscovado sugar
150 ml/¼ pint chicken stock
1½ tsp clear honey
8 tsp cornflour

450 ml/¾ pint groundnut
    oil for frying
1 medium egg
To garnish:
fresh sprigs of dill
orange wedges

Remove and discard any fat and sinew from the pork fillet, then cut into 2 cm/¾ inch cubes and place in a shallow dish. Blend the light soy sauce with the dry sherry and add seasoning. Pour over the pork and stir until the pork is lightly coated. Cover and leave to marinate in the refrigerator for at least 30 minutes, stirring occasionally.

Meanwhile, blend the sherry vinegar, tomato paste, dark soy sauce, light muscovado sugar, chicken stock and honey together in a small saucepan and heat gently, stirring occasionally, until the sugar has dissolved. Then bring to the boil.

Blend 2 teaspoons of cornflour with 1 tablespoon of water and stir into the sauce. Cook, stirring, until smooth and thickened, and either keep warm or reheat when required.

Heat the oil in the wok to 190˚C/375˚F. Whisk together the remaining 6 teaspoons of cornflour and the egg to make a smooth batter. Drain the pork if necessary, then dip the pieces into the batter, allowing any excess to drip back into the bowl. Cook in the hot oil for 2–3 minutes, or until golden and tender. Drain on kitchen paper. Cook the pork in batches until it is all cooked, then garnish and serve immediately with the sauce.

Try this: FOR AN ALTERNATIVE: 250   FOR ENTERTAINING: 254

Speedy Pork with Yellow Bean Sauce

SERVES 4

450 g/1 lb pork fillet
2 tbsp light soy sauce
2 tbsp orange juice
2 tsp cornflour
3 tbsp groundnut oil
2 garlic cloves, peeled and

crushed
175 g/6 oz carrots, peeled
and cut into matchsticks
125 g/4 oz fine green beans,
trimmed and halved
2 spring onions, trimmed

and cut into strips
4 tbsp yellow bean sauce
1 tbsp freshly chopped flat
leaf parsley, to garnish
freshly cooked egg noodles,
to serve

Remove any fat or sinew from the pork fillet, and cut into thin strips. Blend the soy sauce, orange juice and cornflour in a bowl and mix thoroughly. Place the meat in a shallow dish, pour over the soy sauce mixture, cover and leave to marinate in the refrigerator for 1 hour. Drain with a slotted spoon, reserving the marinade.

Heat the wok, then add 2 tablespoons of the oil and stir-fry the pork with the garlic for 2 minutes, or until the meat is sealed. Remove with a slotted spoon and reserve.

Add the remaining oil to the wok and cook the carrots, beans and spring onions for about 3 minutes, until tender but still crisp. Return the pork to the wok with the reserved marinade, then pour over the yellow bean sauce. Stir-fry for a further 1–2 minutes, or until the pork is tender. Sprinkle with the chopped parsley and serve immediately with freshly cooked egg noodles.

Try this: FOR AN ALTERNATIVE: 198   FOR ENTERTAINING: 272

Honey Pork with Rice Noodles & Cashews

SERVES 4

125 g/4 oz rice noodles
450 g/1 lb pork fillet
2 tbsp groundnut oil
1 tbsp softened butter
1 onion, peeled and finely
  sliced into rings
2 garlic cloves, peeled and
  crushed
125 g/4 oz baby button
  mushrooms, halved
3 tbsp light soy sauce
3 tbsp clear honey
50 g/2 oz unsalted
  cashew nuts
1 red chilli, deseeded and
  finely chopped
4 spring onions, trimmed
  and finely chopped
freshly stir-fried vegetables,
  to serve

Soak the rice noodles in boiling water for 4 minutes or according to packet instructions, then drain and reserve.

Trim and slice the pork fillet into thin strips. Heat the wok, pour in the oil and butter, and stir-fry the pork for 4–5 minutes, until cooked. Remove with a slotted spoon and keep warm.

Add the onion to the wok and stir-fry gently for 2 minutes. Stir in the garlic and mushrooms and cook for a further 2 minutes, or until juices start to run from the mushrooms.

Blend the soy sauce with the honey then return the pork to the wok with this mixture. Add the cashew nuts and cook for 1–2 minutes, then add the rice noodles a little at a time. Stir-fry until everything is piping hot. Sprinkle with chopped chilli and spring onions. Serve immediately with freshly stir-fried vegetables.

Try this: FOR AN ALTERNATIVE: 258 FOR ENTERTAINING: 280

Sweet & Sour Pork

SERVES 4

450 g/1 lb pork fillet
1 medium egg white
4 tsp cornflour
salt and freshly ground
    black pepper
300 ml/½ pint groundnut oil
1 small onion, peeled and
    finely sliced

125 g/4 oz carrots, peeled
    and cut into matchsticks
2.5 cm/1 inch piece fresh
    root ginger, peeled and
    cut into thin strips
150 ml/¼ pint orange juice
150 ml/¼ pint chicken stock
1 tbsp light soy sauce

220 g can pineapple pieces,
    drained with juice
    reserved
1 tbsp white wine vinegar
1 tbsp freshly
    chopped parsley
freshly cooked rice,
    to serve

Trim the pork fillet then cut into small cubes. In a bowl, whisk the egg white and cornflour with a little seasoning, then add the pork to the egg white mixture and stir until the cubes are well coated.

Heat the wok, then add the oil and heat until very hot before adding the pork and stir-frying for 30 seconds. Turn off the heat and continue to stir for 3 minutes. The meat should be white and sealed. Drain off the oil, reserve the pork and wipe the wok clean.

Pour 2 teaspoons of the drained groundnut oil back into the wok and cook the onion, carrots and ginger for 2–3 minutes. Blend the orange juice with the chicken stock and soy sauce and make up to 300 ml/½ pint with the reserved pineapple juice.

Return the pork to the wok with the juice mixture and simmer for 3–4 minutes. Then stir in the pineapple pieces and vinegar. Heat through, then sprinkle with the chopped parsley and serve immediately with freshly cooked rice.

Try this: FOR AN ALTERNATIVE: 202 FOR ENTERTAINING: 214

Pork in Peanut Sauce

SERVES 4

450 g/1 lb pork fillet
2 tbsp light soy sauce
1 tbsp vinegar
1 tsp sugar
1 tsp Chinese five
  spice powder
2–4 garlic cloves, peeled
  and crushed
2 tbsp groundnut oil

1 large onion, peeled and
  finely sliced
125 g/4 oz carrots, peeled
  and cut into matchsticks
2 celery sticks, trimmed
  and sliced
125 g/4 oz French beans,
  trimmed and halved
3 tbsp smooth peanut butter

1 tbsp freshly chopped flat
  leaf parsley

To serve:
freshly cooked basmati
  and wild rice
green salad

Remove any fat or sinew from the pork fillet, cut into thin strips and reserve. Blend the soy sauce, vinegar, sugar, Chinese five spice powder and garlic in a bowl and add the pork. Cover and leave to marinate in the refrigerator for at least 30 minutes.

Drain the pork, reserving any marinade. Heat the wok, then add the oil and, when hot, stir-fry the pork for 3–4 minutes, or until sealed.

Add the onion, carrots, celery and beans to the wok and stir-fry for 4–5 minutes, or until the meat is tender and the vegetables are softened.

Blend the reserved marinade, the peanut butter and 2 tablespoons of hot water together. When smooth, stir into the wok and cook for several minutes more until the sauce is thick and the pork is piping hot. Sprinkle with the chopped parsley and serve immediately with the basmati and wild rice and a green salad.

Try this: FOR AN ALTERNATIVE: 280   FOR ENTERTAINING: 254

Pork with Spring Vegetables & Sweet Chilli Sauce

SERVES 4

450 g/16 oz pork fillet
2 tbsp sunflower oil
2 garlic cloves,
    peeled and crushed
2.5 cm/1 inch piece fresh
    root ginger, peeled
    and grated

125 g/4 oz carrots, peeled
    and cut into matchsticks
4 spring onions, trimmed
125 g/4 oz sugar snap peas
125 g/4 oz baby sweetcorn
2 tbsp sweet chilli sauce
2 tbsp light soy sauce

1 tbsp vinegar
½ tsp sugar, or to taste
125 g/4 oz beansprouts
grated zest of 1 orange
freshly cooked rice,
    to serve

Trim, then cut the pork fillet into thin strips and reserve. Heat a wok and pour in the oil. When hot, add the garlic and ginger and stir-fry for 30 seconds. Add the carrots to the wok and continue to stir-fry for 1–2 minute, or until they start to soften.

Slice the spring onions lengthways, then cut into 3 lengths. Trim the sugar snap peas and the sweetcorn. Add the spring onions, sugar snap peas and sweetcorn to the wok and stir-fry for 30 seconds.

Add the pork to the wok and continue to stir-fry for 2–3 minutes, or until the meat is sealed and browned all over. Blend the sweet chilli sauce, soy sauce, vinegar and sugar together, then stir into the wok with the beansprouts.

Continue to stir-fry until the meat is cooked and the vegetables are tender but still crisp. Sprinkle with the orange zest and serve immediately with the freshly cooked rice.

Try this: FOR AN ALTERNATIVE: 168   FOR ENTERTAINING: 226

Char Sui Pork & Noodle Salad

SERVES 4

200 g/7 oz flat rice noodles
4 tbsp black treacle
2 tbsp dark soy sauce
3 tbsp Chinese rice wine or
   dry sherry
3 star anise, roughly crushed
1 cinnamon stick
350 g/12 oz pork tenderloin,

in 1 piece
1 tbsp groundnut oil
2 garlic cloves, peeled
   and finely chopped
1 tsp freshly grated
   root ginger
3 spring onions,
   trimmed and sliced

125 g/4 oz pak choi,
   roughly chopped
2 tbsp light soy sauce
fresh coriander leaves,
   to garnish
prepared or bought plum
   sauce, to serve

Preheat the oven to 220°C/425°F/Gas Mark 7, 15 minutes before cooking. Soak the noodles in boiling water according to the packet directions. Drain and reserve. Place the treacle, soy sauce, Chinese rice wine or sherry, star anise and cinnamon into a small saucepan and stir over a gentle heat until mixed thoroughly, then reserve.

Trim the pork tenderloin of any excess fat and put into a shallow dish. Pour the cooled sauce over the tenderloin. Turn the pork, making sure it is completely coated in the sauce. Place in the refrigerator and leave to marinate for 4 hours, turning occasionally. Remove the pork from its marinade and transfer to a roasting tin. Roast in the preheated oven for 12–14 minutes, basting once, until the pork is cooked through. Remove from the oven and leave until just warm.

Heat the wok, add the oil and when hot, add the garlic, ginger and spring onions. Stir-fry for 30 seconds before adding the pak choi. Stir-fry for a further 1 minute until the pak choi has wilted, then add the noodles and soy sauce. Toss for a few seconds until well mixed, then transfer to a large serving dish. Leave to cool. Thickly slice the pork fillet and add to the cooled noodles. Garnish with coriander leaves and serve with plum sauce.

Try this: FOR AN ALTERNATIVE: 194   FOR ENTERTAINING: 206

Chinese Bean Sauce Noodles

SERVES 4

250 g/9oz fine egg noodles
1½ tbsp sesame oil
1 tbsp groundnut oil
3 garlic cloves, peeled and
    finely chopped
4 spring onions, trimmed

and finely chopped
450 g/1 lb fresh pork mince
100 ml/4 fl oz crushed yellow
    bean sauce
1-2 tsp hot chilli sauce
1 tbsp Chinese rice wine or

dry sherry
2 tbsp dark soy sauce
½ tsp cayenne pepper
2 tsp sugar
150 ml/¼ pint chicken stock

Put the noodles into a large bowl and pour over boiling water to cover. Leave to soak according to packet directions until tender. Drain well and place in a bowl with the sesame oil. Toss together well and reserve.

Heat a wok until it is hot, add the groundnut oil and when it is hot, add the garlic and half the spring onions. Stir-fry for a few seconds, then add the pork. Stir well to break up and continue to stir-fry for 1–2 minutes until it changes colour.

Add the yellow bean sauce, chilli sauce, Chinese rice wine or sherry, soy sauce, cayenne pepper, sugar and chicken stock, stirring all the time. Bring to the boil, reduce the heat and simmer for 5 minutes.

Meanwhile, bring a large saucepan of water to the boil and add the noodles for about 20 seconds. Drain well and tip into a warmed serving bowl. Pour the sauce over the top, sprinkle with the remaining spring onions and mix well. Serve immediately.

Try this: FOR AN ALTERNATIVE: 192   FOR ENTERTAINING: 310

Pork Meatballs with Vegetables

SERVES 4

450 g/1 lb pork mince
2 tbsp freshly
    chopped coriander
2 garlic cloves,
    peeled and chopped
1 tbsp light soy sauce
salt and freshly ground
    black pepper
2 tbsp groundnut oil

2 cm/1 inch piece fresh root
    ginger, peeled and cut
    into matchsticks
1 red pepper, deseeded and
    cut into chunks
1 green pepper, deseeded
    and cut into chunks
2 courgettes, trimmed and
    cut into sticks

125 g/4 oz baby sweetcorn,
    halved lengthways
3 tbsp light soy sauce
1 tsp sesame oil
fresh coriander leaves,
    to garnish
freshly cooked noodles,
    to serve

Mix together the pork mince, the chopped coriander, half the garlic and the soy sauce, then season to taste with salt and pepper. Divide into 20 portions and roll into balls. Place on a baking sheet, cover with clingfilm and chill in the refrigerator for at least 30 minutes.

Heat a wok or large frying pan, add the groundnut oil and when hot, add the meatballs and cook for 8–10 minutes, or until the pork balls are browned all over, turning occasionally. Using a slotted spoon, transfer the balls to a plate and keep warm.

Add the ginger and remaining garlic to the wok and stir-fry for 30 seconds. Add the red and green peppers and stir-fry for 5 minutes. Add the courgettes and sweetcorn and stir-fry for 3 minutes.

Return the pork balls to the wok, add the soy sauce and sesame oil and stir-fry for 1 minute, until heated through. Garnish with coriander leaves and serve immediately on a bed of noodles.

Try this: FOR AN ALTERNATIVE: 218   FOR ENTERTAINING: 168

Lamb with Stir-fried Vegetables

SERVES 4

550 g/1¼ lb lamb fillet,
    cut into strips
2.5 cm/1 inch piece fresh
    root ginger, peeled and
    cut into matchsticks
2 garlic cloves,
    peeled and chopped
4 tbsp soy sauce
2 tbsp dry sherry

2 tsp cornflour
4 tbsp groundnut oil
75 g/3 oz French beans,
    trimmed and cut in half
2 medium carrots, peeled
    and cut into matchsticks
1 red pepper, deseeded and
    cut into chunks
1 yellow pepper, deseeded

and cut into chunks
225 g can water chestnuts,
    drained and halved
3 tomatoes, chopped
freshly cooked sticky rice
    in banana leaves,
    to serve (optional)

Place the lamb strips in a shallow dish. Mix together the ginger and half the garlic in a small bowl. Pour over the soy sauce and sherry and stir well. Pour over the lamb and stir until coated lightly. Cover with clingfilm and leave to marinate for at least 30 minutes, occasionally spooning the marinade over the lamb.

Using a slotted spoon, lift the lamb from the marinade and place on a plate. Blend the cornflour and the marinade together until smooth and reserve.

Heat a wok or large frying pan, add 2 tablespoons of the oil and when hot, add the remaining garlic, French beans, carrots and peppers and stir-fry for 5 minutes. Using a slotted spoon, transfer the vegetables to a plate and keep warm.

Heat the remaining oil in the wok, add the lamb and stir-fry for 2 minutes or until tender. Return the vegetables to the wok with the water chestnuts, tomatoes and reserved marinade mixture. Bring to the boil then simmer for 1 minute. Serve immediately with freshly cooked sticky rice in banana leaves, if liked.

 Try this: FOR AN ALTERNATIVE: 290   FOR ENTERTAINING: 304

Lamb with Black Cherry Sauce

SERVES 4

550 g/1¼ lb lamb fillet
2 tbsp light soy sauce
1 tsp Chinese five
   spice powder
4 tbsp fresh orange juice
175 g/6 oz black cherry jam

150 ml/¼ pint red wine
50 g/2 oz fresh black cherries
1 tbsp groundnut oil
1 tbsp freshly
   chopped coriander,
   to garnish

To serve:
thawed frozen peas
freshly cooked noodles

Remove the skin and any fat from the lamb fillet and cut into thin slices. Place in a shallow dish. Mix together the soy sauce, Chinese five spice powder and orange juice and pour over the meat. Cover and leave in the refrigerator for at least 30 minutes.

Meanwhile, blend the jam and the wine together, pour into a small saucepan and bring to the boil. Simmer gently for 10 minutes until slightly thickened. Remove the stones from the cherries, using a cherry stoner if possible in order to keep them whole.

Drain the lamb when ready to cook. Heat the wok, add the oil and when the oil is hot, stir-fry the slices of lamb for 3–5 minutes, or until just slightly pink inside or cooked to personal preference.

Spoon the lamb into a warm serving dish and serve immediately with a little of the cherry sauce drizzled over. Garnish with the chopped coriander and the whole cherries and serve immediately with peas, freshly cooked noodles and the remaining sauce.

Try this: FOR AN ALTERNATIVE: 334   FOR ENTERTAINING: 328

Chilli Lamb

SERVES 4

550 g/1¼ lb lamb fillet
3 tbsp groundnut oil
1 large onion, peeled
    and finely sliced
2 garlic cloves,
    peeled and crushed

4 tsp cornflour
4 tbsp hot chilli sauce
2 tbsp white wine vinegar
4 tsp dark soft brown sugar
1 tsp Chinese five
    spice powder

sprigs of fresh coriander,
    to garnish

To serve:
freshly cooked noodles
4 tbsp Greek style yogurt

Trim the lamb fillet, discarding any fat or sinew, then place it on a clean chopping board and cut into thin strips. Heat a wok and pour in 2 tablespoons of the groundnut oil and when hot, stir-fry the lamb for 3–4 minutes, or until it is browned. Remove the lamb strips with their juices and reserve.

Add the remaining oil to the wok, then stir-fry the onion and garlic for 2 minutes, or until softened. Remove with a slotted spoon and add to the lamb.

Blend the cornflour with 125 ml/4 fl oz of cold water, then stir in the chilli sauce, vinegar, sugar and Chinese five spice powder. Pour this into the wok, turn up the heat and bring the mixture to the boil. Cook for 30 seconds or until the sauce thickens.

Return the lamb to the wok with the onion and garlic, stir thoroughly and heat through until piping hot. Garnish with sprigs of fresh coriander and serve immediately with freshly cooked noodles, topped with a spoonful of Greek yogurt.

Try this: FOR AN ALTERNATIVE: 166   FOR ENTERTAINING: 176

Kung-pao Lamb

SERVES 4

450 g/1 lb lamb fillet
2 tbsp soy sauce
2 tbsp Chinese rice wine
   or dry sherry
2 tbsp sunflower oil
2 tsp sesame oil
50 g/2 oz unsalted peanuts
1 garlic clove, peeled
   and crushed

2.5 cm/1 inch piece
   fresh root ginger,
   finely chopped
1 red chilli, deseeded and
   finely chopped
1 small green pepper,
   deseeded and diced
6 spring onions, trimmed
   and diagonally sliced

125 ml/4 fl oz lamb or
   vegetable stock
1 tsp red wine vinegar
1 tsp soft light brown sugar
2 tsp cornflour
plain boiled or steamed
   white rice, to serve

Wrap the lamb in baking parchment paper and place in the freezer for about 30 minutes until stiff. Cut the meat across the grain into paper-thin slices. Put in a shallow bowl, add 2 teaspoons of the soy sauce and all the Chinese rice wine or sherry and leave to marinate in the refrigerator for 15 minutes.

Heat a wok or frying pan until hot, add the sunflower oil and swirl it around to coat the sides. Add the lamb and stir-fry for about 1 minute until lightly browned. Remove from the wok or pan and reserve, leaving any juices behind.

Add the sesame oil to the wok or pan and stir-fry the peanuts, garlic, ginger, chilli, green pepper and spring onions for 1–2 minutes, or until the nuts are golden. Return the lamb with the remaining soy sauce, stock, vinegar and sugar.

Blend the cornflour with 1 tablespoon of water. Stir in and cook the mixture for 1–2 minutes, or until the vegetables are tender and the sauce has thickened. Serve immediately with plain boiled or steamed white rice.

Try this: FOR AN ALTERNATIVE: 230 FOR ENTERTAINING: 228

Asian Food: Poultry

Soy-glazed Chicken Thighs

SERVES 6-8

900 g/2 lb chicken thighs
2 tbsp vegetable oil
3–4 garlic cloves, peeled
   and crushed
4 cm/1½ inch piece fresh
   root ginger, peeled and

finely chopped or grated
125 ml/4 fl oz soy sauce
2–3 tbsp Chinese rice wine
   or dry sherry
2 tbsp clear honey
1 tbsp soft brown sugar

2–3 dashes hot chilli sauce,
   or to taste
freshly chopped parsley,
   to garnish

Heat a large wok and when hot, add the oil and heat. Stir-fry the chicken thighs for 5 minutes or until golden. Remove and drain on absorbent kitchen paper. You may need to do this in 2–3 batches.

Pour off the oil and fat and, using absorbent kitchen paper, carefully wipe out the wok. Add the garlic, with the root ginger, soy sauce, Chinese rice wine or sherry and honey to the wok and stir well. Sprinkle in the soft brown sugar with the hot chilli sauce to taste, then place over the heat and bring to the boil.

Reduce the heat to a gentle simmer, then carefully add the chicken thighs. Cover the wok and simmer gently over a very low heat for 30 minutes, or until they are tender and the sauce is reduced and thickened and glazes the chicken thighs.

Stir or spoon the sauce occasionally over the chicken thighs and add a little water if the sauce is starting to become too thick. Arrange in a shallow serving dish, garnish with freshly chopped parsley and serve immediately.

Try this: FOR AN ALTERNATIVE: 344   FOR ENTERTAINING: 278

Chinese Chicken Soup

SERVES 4

225 g/8 oz cooked chicken
1 tsp oil
6 spring onions, trimmed
and diagonally sliced
1 red chilli, deseeded
and finely chopped
1 garlic clove, peeled

and crushed
2.5 cm/1 inch piece
root ginger, peeled
and finely grated
1 litre/1¾ pint chicken stock
150 g/5 oz medium
egg noodles

1 carrot, peeled and cut
into matchsticks
125 g/4 oz beansprouts
2 tbsp soy sauce
1 tbsp fish sauce
fresh coriander leaves,
to garnish

Remove any skin from the chicken. Place on a chopping board and use two forks to tear the chicken into fine shreds.

Heat the oil in a large saucepan and fry the spring onions and chilli for 1 minute. Add the garlic and ginger and cook for another minute.

Stir in the chicken stock and gradually bring the mixture to the boil. Break up the noodles a little and add to the boiling stock with the carrot.

Stir to mix, then reduce the heat to a simmer and cook for 3–4 minutes. Add the shredded chicken, beansprouts, soy sauce and fish sauce and stir.

Cook for a further 2–3 minutes until piping hot. Ladle the soup into bowls and sprinkle with the coriander leaves. Serve immediately.

 Try this: FOR AN ALTERNATIVE: 150   FOR ENTERTAINING: 184

Coriander Chicken & Soy Sauce Cakes

SERVES 4

¼ cucumber, peeled
1 shallot, peeled and thinly sliced
6 radishes, trimmed and sliced
350 g/12 oz skinless boneless chicken thigh

4 tbsp roughly chopped fresh coriander
2 spring onions, trimmed and roughly chopped
1 red chilli, deseeded and chopped
finely grated rind of ½ lime

2 tbsp soy sauce
1 tbsp caster sugar
2 tbsp rice vinegar
1 red chilli, deseeded and finely sliced
freshly chopped coriander, to garnish

Preheat the oven to 190°C/375°F/Gas Mark 5. Halve the cucumber lengthwise, deseed and dice. In a bowl mix the shallot and radishes. Chill until ready to serve with the diced cucumber.

Place the chicken thighs in a food processor and blend until coarsely chopped. Add the coriander and spring onions to the chicken with the chilli, lime rind and soy sauce. Blend again until mixed.

Using slightly damp hands, shape the chicken mixture into 12 small rounds. Place the rounds on a lightly oiled baking tray and bake in the preheated for 15 minutes, until golden.

In a small pan heat the sugar with 2 tablespoons of water until dissolved. Simmer until syrupy. Remove from the heat and allow to cool a little, then stir in the vinegar and chilli slices. Pour over the cucumber and the radish and shallot salad.

Garnish with the chopped coriander and serve the chicken cakes with the salad immediately.

Try this: FOR AN ALTERNATIVE: 200   FOR ENTERTAINING: 344

Wonton Soup

SERVES 6

For the chicken stock:
900 g/2 lb chicken or
   chicken pieces with back,
   feet and wings
1–2 onions,
   peeled and quartered
2 carrots,
   peeled and chopped
2 celery stalks,
   trimmed and chopped
1 leek, trimmed and chopped
2 garlic cloves, unpeeled

and lightly crushed
1 tbsp black peppercorns
2 bay leaves
small bunch parsley,
   stems only
2–3 slices fresh root ginger,
   peeled (optional)
3.4 litres/6 pints cold water

For the soup:
18 wontons
2–3 Chinese leaves, or a

handful of spinach,
   shredded
1 small carrot, peeled and
   cut into matchsticks
2–4 spring onions, trimmed
   and diagonally sliced
soy sauce, to taste
handful flat leaf parsley,
   to garnish

Chop the duck into six to eight pieces and put into a large stock pot or saucepan of water with the remaining stock ingredients. Place over a high heat and bring to the boil, skimming off any scum which rises to the surface. Reduce the heat and simmer for 2–3 hours, skimming occasionally. Strain the stock through a fine sieve or muslin-lined sieve into a large bowl. Leave to cool, then chill in the refrigerator for 5–6 hours, or overnight. When cold, skim off the fat and remove any small pieces of fat by dragging a piece of absorbent kitchen paper lightly across the surface.

Bring a medium saucepan of water to the boil. Add the wontons and return to the boil. Simmer for 2–3 minutes, or until the wontons are cooked, stir frequently. Rinse under cold running water, drain and reserve. Pour 300 ml/½ pint stock per person into a large wok. Bring to the boil over a high heat, skimming off any foam that rises to the surface and simmer for 5–7 minutes to reduce slightly. Add the wontons, Chinese leaves or spinach, carrots and spring onions. Season with a few drops of soy sauce and simmer for 2–3 minutes. Garnish with a few parsley leaves and serve immediately.

Try this: FOR AN ALTERNATIVE: 184   FOR ENTERTAINING: 186

Oriental Minced Chicken on Rocket & Tomato

SERVES 4

2 shallots, peeled
1 garlic clove, peeled
1 carrot, peeled
50 g/2 oz water chestnuts
1 tsp oil

350 g/12 oz fresh
   chicken mince
1 tsp Chinese five
   spice powder
pinch chilli powder

1 tsp soy sauce
1 tbsp fish sauce
8 cherry tomatoes
50 g/2 oz rocket

Finely chop the shallots and garlic. Cut the carrot into matchsticks, thinly slice the water chestnuts and reserve. Heat the oil in a wok or heavy-based large frying pan and add the chicken. Stir-fry for 3–4 minutes over a moderately high heat, breaking up any large pieces of chicken.

Add the garlic and shallots and cook for 2–3 minutes until softened. Sprinkle over the Chinese 5-spice powder and the chilli powder and continue to cook for about 1 minute.

Add the carrot, water chestnuts, soy and fish sauce and 2 tablespoons of water. Stir-fry for a further 2 minutes. Remove from the heat and reserve to cool slightly.

Deseed the tomatoes and cut into thin wedges. Toss with the rocket and divide between four serving plates. Spoon the warm chicken mixture over the rocket and tomato wedges and serve immediately to prevent the rocket from wilting.

Try this: FOR AN ALTERNATIVE: 84   FOR ENTERTAINING: 240

Hot & Sour Soup

SERVES 4-6

25 g/1 oz dried Chinese (shiitake) mushrooms
2 tbsp groundnut oil
1 carrot, peeled and cut into julienne strips
125 g/4 oz chestnut mushrooms, wiped and thinly sliced
2 garlic cloves, peeled and finely chopped

½ tsp dried crushed chillies
1.1 litres/2 pints chicken stock
75 g/3 oz cooked, boneless chicken or pork, shredded
125 g/4 oz fresh bean curd, thinly sliced, optional
2–3 spring onions, trimmed and finely sliced diagonally

1–2 tsp sugar
3 tbsp cider vinegar
2 tbsp soy sauce
salt and freshly ground black pepper
1 tbsp cornflour
1 large egg
2 tsp sesame oil
2 tbsp freshly chopped coriander

Place the dried Chinese (shiitake) mushrooms in a small bowl and pour over enough almost boiling water to cover. Leave for 20 minutes to soften, then gently lift out and squeeze out the liquid. (Lifting out the mushrooms leaves any sand and grit behind.) Discard the stems and thinly slice the caps and reserve.

Heat a large wok, add the oil and when hot, add the carrot strips and stir-fry for 2–3 minutes, or until beginning to soften. Add the chestnut mushrooms and stir-fry for 2–3 minutes, or until golden, then stir in the garlic and chillies. Add the chicken stock to the vegetables and bring to the boil, skimming any foam which rises to the surface. Add the shredded chicken or pork, bean curd, if using, spring onions, sugar, vinegar, soy sauce and reserved Chinese mushrooms and simmer for 5 minutes, stirring occasionally. Season to taste with salt and pepper.

Blend the cornflour with 1 tablespoon of cold water to form a smooth paste and whisk into the soup. Return to the boil and simmer over a medium heat until thickened. Beat the egg with the sesame oil and slowly add to the soup in a slow, steady stream, stirring constantly. Stir in the chopped coriander and serve the soup immediately.

Try this: FOR AN ALTERNATIVE: 346 FOR ENTERTAINING: 238

Laksa Malayan Rice Noodle Soup

SERVES 4-6

1.1 kg/2½ lb corn-fed, free-range chicken
1 tsp black peppercorns
1 tbsp vegetable oil
1 large onion, peeled and thinly sliced
2 garlic cloves, peeled and finely chopped
2.5 cm/1 inch piece fresh root ginger, peeled and thinly sliced
1 tsp ground coriander
2 red chillies, deseeded and diagonally sliced
1–2 tsp hot curry paste
400 ml/14 fl oz coconut milk
450 g/1 lb large raw prawns, peeled and de-veined
½ small head of Chinese leaves, thinly shredded
1 tsp sugar
2 spring onions, trimmed and thinly sliced
125 g/4 oz beansprouts
250 g/9 oz rice noodles or rice sticks, soaked as per packet instructions
fresh mint leaves, to garnish

Put the chicken in a large saucepan with the peppercorns and cover with cold water. Bring to the boil, skimming off any scum that rises to the surface. Simmer, partially covered, for about 1 hour. Remove the chicken and cool. Skim any fat from the stock and strain through a muslin-lined sieve and reserve. Remove the meat from the carcass, shred and reserve.

Heat a large wok, add the oil and when hot, add the onions and stir-fry for 2 minutes, or until they begin to colour. Stir in the garlic, ginger, coriander, chillies and curry paste and stir-fry for a further 2 minutes. Carefully pour in the reserved stock (you need at least 1.1 litres/2 pints) and simmer gently, partially covered, for 10 minutes, or until slightly reduced.

Add the coconut milk, prawns, Chinese leaves, sugar, spring onions and beansprouts and simmer for 3 minutes, stirring occasionally. Add the reserved shredded chicken, and cook for a further 2 minutes. Drain the noodles and divide between four to six soup bowls. Ladle the hot stock and vegetables over the noodles, making sure each serving has some prawns and chicken. Garnish each bowl with fresh mint leaves and serve immediately.

Try this: FOR AN ALTERNATIVE: 68 FOR ENTERTAINING: 82

Chicken–filled Spring Rolls

MAKES 12-14 ROLLS

For the filling:
1 tbsp vegetable oil
2 slices streaky bacon, diced
225 g/8 oz skinless chicken
    breast fillets, thinly sliced
1 small red pepper,deseeded
    and finely chopped
4 spring onions, trimmed
    and finely chopped
2.5 cm/1 inch piece fresh

root ginger, peeled and
    finely chopped
75 g/3 oz mangetout peas,
    thinly sliced
75 g/3 oz beansprouts
1 tbsp soy sauce
2 tsp Chinese rice wine
    or dry sherry
2 tsp hoisin or plum sauce

For the wrappers:
3 tbsp plain flour
12–14 spring roll wrappers
300 ml/½ pint vegetable oil
    for deep frying
shredded spring onions,
    to garnish
dipping sauce,
    to serve

Heat a large wok, add the oil and when hot add the diced bacon and stir-fry for 2–3 minutes, or until golden. Add the chicken and pepper and stir-fry for a further 2–3 minutes. Add the remaining filling ingredients and stir-fry 3–4 minutes until all the vegetables are tender. Turn into a colander and leave to drain as the mixture cools completely.

Blend the flour with about 1½ tablespoons of water to form a paste. Soften each wrapper in a plate of warm water for 1–2 seconds, then place on a chopping board. Put 2–3 tablespoons of filling on the near edge. Fold the edge over the filling to cover. Fold in each side and roll up. Seal the edge with a little flour paste and press to seal securely. Transfer to a baking sheet, seam-side down.

Heat the oil in a large wok to 190°C/375°F, or until a small cube of bread browns in about 30 seconds. Working in batches of 3–4, fry the spring rolls until they are crisp and golden, turning once (about 2 minutes). Remove and drain on absorbent kitchen paper. Arrange the spring rolls on a serving plate, garnish with spring onion tassels and serve hot with dipping sauce.

Try this: FOR AN ALTERNATIVE: 376   FOR ENTERTAINING: 200

Spicy Chicken Skewers with Mango Tabbouleh

SERVES 4

400 g/14 oz chicken
breast fillet
200 ml/7 fl oz natural
low fat yogurt
1 garlic clove, peeled
and crushed
1 small red chilli, deseeded
and finely chopped
½ tsp ground turmeric

finely grated rind and juice
of ½ lemon
sprigs of fresh mint,
to garnish

For the mango tabbouleh:
175 g/6 oz bulgur wheat
1 tsp olive oil
juice of ½ lemon

½ red onion, finely chopped
1 ripe mango, halved, stoned,
peeled and chopped
¼ cucumber, finely diced
2 tbsp freshly
chopped parsley
2 tbsp freshly shredded mint
salt and finely ground
black pepper

If using wooden skewers, pre-soak them in cold water for at least 30 minutes – this stops them from burning during grilling.

Cut the chicken into 5 x 1 cm/2 x ½ inch strips and place in a shallow dish. Mix together the yogurt, garlic, chilli, turmeric, lemon rind and juice. Pour over the chicken and toss to coat. Cover and leave to marinate in the refrigerator for up to 8 hours.

To make the tabbouleh, put the bulgur wheat in a bowl. Pour over enough boiling water to cover. Put a plate over the bowl. Leave to soak for 20 minutes. Whisk together the oil and lemon juice in a bowl. Add the red onion and leave to marinade for 10 minutes. Drain the bulgur wheat and squeeze out any excess moisture in a clean tea towel. Add to the red onion with the mango, cucumber, herbs and season to taste with salt and pepper. Toss together.

Thread the chicken strips on to eight wooden or metal skewers. Cook under a hot grill for 8 minutes. Turn and brush with the marinade, until the chicken is lightly browned and cooked through. Spoon the tabbouleh on to individual plates. Arrange the chicken skewers on top and garnish with the sprigs of mint. Serve warm or cold.

Try this: FOR AN ALTERNATIVE: 244   FOR ENTERTAINING: 344

Chicken & Lamb Satay

MAKES 16

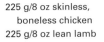

225 g/8 oz skinless,
   boneless chicken
225 g/8 oz lean lamb

For the marinade:
1 small onion, peeled
   and finely chopped
2 garlic cloves, peeled
   and crushed
2.5 cm/1 inch piece fresh
   root ginger, peeled

and grated
4 tbsp soy sauce
1 tsp ground coriander
2 tsp dark brown sugar
2 tbsp lime juice
1 tbsp vegetable oil

For the peanut sauce:
300 ml/½ pint coconut milk
4 tbsp crunchy peanut butter
1 tbsp Thai fish sauce

1 tsp lime juice
1 tbsp chilli powder
1 tbsp brown sugar
salt and freshly ground
   black pepper

To garnish:
sprigs of fresh coriander
lime wedges

Preheat the grill just before cooking. Soak the bamboo skewers for 30 minutes before required. Cut the chicken and lamb into thin strips, about 7.5 cm/3 inches long and place in two shallow dishes. Blend all the marinade ingredients together, then pour half over the chicken and half over the lamb. Stir until lightly coated, then cover with clingfilm and leave to marinate in the refrigerator for at least 2 hours, turning occasionally.

Remove the chicken and lamb from the marinade and thread on to the skewers. Reserve the marinade. Cook under the preheated grill for 8–10 minutes or until cooked, turning and brushing with the marinade.

Meanwhile, make the peanut sauce. Blend the coconut milk with the peanut butter, fish sauce, lime juice, chilli powder and sugar. Pour into a saucepan and cook gently for 5 minutes, stirring occasionally, then season to taste with salt and pepper. Garnish with coriander sprigs and lime wedges and serve the satays with the prepared sauce.

Try this: FOR AN ALTERNATIVE: 236   FOR ENTERTAINING: 194

Sweet & Sour Rice with Chicken

SERVES 4

4 spring onions	1 garlic clove,	4 tbsp tomato ketchup
2 tsp sesame oil	peeled and crushed	1 tbsp tomato purée
1 tsp Chinese	1 medium onion, peeled and	2 tbsp honey
five spice powder	sliced into thin wedges	1 tbsp vinegar
450 g/1 lb chicken breast,	225 g/8 oz long-grain	1 tbsp dark soy sauce
cut into cubes	white rice	1 carrot, peeled and
1 tbsp oil	600 ml/1 pint water	cut into matchsticks

Trim the spring onions, then cut lengthways into fine strips. Drop into a large bowl of iced water and reserve.

Mix together the sesame oil and Chinese five spice powder and use to rub into the cubed chicken. Heat the wok, then add the oil and when hot, cook the garlic and onion for 2–3 minutes, or until transparent and softened.

Add the chicken and stir-fry over a medium-high heat until the chicken is golden and cooked through. Using a slotted spoon, remove from the wok and keep warm.

Stir the rice into the wok and add the water, tomato ketchup, tomato purée, honey, vinegar and soy sauce. Stir well to mix. Bring to the boil, then simmer until almost all of the liquid is absorbed. Stir in the carrot and reserved chicken and continue to cook for 3–4 minutes.

Drain the spring onions, which will have become curly. Garnish with the spring onion curls and serve immediately with the rice and chicken.

Try this: FOR AN ALTERNATIVE: 214   FOR ENTERTAINING: 290

Pan–cooked Chicken with Thai Spices

SERVES 4

4 kaffir lime leaves
5 cm/2 inch piece of
root ginger, peeled
and chopped
300 ml/½ pint chicken
stock, boiling
4 x 175 g/6 oz
chicken breasts

2 tsp groundnut oil
5 tbsp coconut milk
1 tbsp fish sauce
2 red chillies, deseeded
and finely chopped
225 g/8 oz Thai jasmine rice
1 tbsp lime juice
3 tbsp freshly

chopped coriander
salt and freshly ground
black pepper

To garnish:
wedges of lime
freshly chopped coriander

Lightly bruise the kaffir lime leaves and put in a bowl with the chopped ginger. Pour over the chicken stock, cover and leave to infuse for 30 minutes.

Meanwhile, cut each chicken breast into two pieces. Heat the oil in a large, non-stick frying pan or flameproof casserole dish and brown the chicken pieces for 2–3 minutes on each side.

Strain the infused chicken stock into the pan. Half cover the pan with a lid and gently simmer for 10 minutes. Stir in the coconut milk, fish sauce and chopped chillies. Simmer, uncovered for 5–6 minutes, or until the chicken is tender and cooked through and the sauce has reduced slightly.

Meanwhile, cook the rice in boiling salted water according to the packet instructions. Drain the rice thoroughly.

Stir the lime juice and chopped coriander into the sauce. Season to taste with salt and pepper. Serve the chicken and sauce on a bed of rice. Garnish with wedges of lime and freshly chopped coriander and serve immediately.

Try this: FOR AN ALTERNATIVE: 196   FOR ENTERTAINING: 144

Cantonese Chicken Wings

SERVES 4

3 tbsp hoisin sauce
2 tbsp dark soy sauce
1 tbsp sesame oil
1 garlic clove, peeled
   and crushed
2.5 cm/1 inch piece fresh
   root ginger, peeled and

   grated
1 tbsp Chinese rice wine
   or dry sherry
2 tsp chilli bean sauce
2 tsp red or white
   wine vinegar
2 tbsp soft light brown sugar

900 g/2 lb large
   chicken wings
50 g/2 oz cashew nuts,
   chopped
2 spring onions, trimmed
   and finely chopped

Preheat the oven to 220°C/425°F/Gas Mark 7, 15 minutes before cooking. Place the hoisin sauce, soy sauce, sesame oil, garlic, ginger, Chinese rice wine or sherry, chilli bean sauce, vinegar and sugar in a small saucepan with 6 tablespoons of water. Bring to the boil, stirring occasionally, then simmer for about 30 seconds. Remove the glaze from the heat.

Place the chicken wings in a roasting tin in a single layer. Pour over the glaze and stir until the wings are coated thoroughly.

Cover the tin loosely with tinfoil, place in the preheated oven and roast for 25 minutes. Remove the tinfoil, baste the wings and cook for a further 5 minutes.

Reduce the oven temperature to 190°C/375°F/Gas Mark 5. Turn the wings over and sprinkle with the chopped cashew nuts and spring onions. Return to the oven and cook for 5 minutes, or until the nuts are lightly browned, the glaze is sticky and the wings are tender.

Remove from the oven and leave to stand for 5 minutes before arranging on a warmed platter. Serve immediately with finger bowls and plenty of napkins.

Try this: FOR AN ALTERNATIVE: 236   FOR ENTERTAINING: 152

Special Fried Rice

SERVES 4

1 large egg
1 tsp sesame oil
350 g/8 oz long-grain
   white rice
1 tbsp groundnut oil
450 g/1 lb boneless, skinless
   chicken breast, diced

8 spring onions, trimmed
   and sliced
2 large carrots, trimmed and
   cut into matchsticks
125 g/4 oz sugar snap peas
125 g/4 oz raw tiger
   prawns, peeled

2 tsp Chinese
   five spice powder
1 tbsp soy sauce
1 tbsp Thai fish sauce
1 tbsp rice wine vinegar

Beat the egg in a bowl with ½ teaspoon of the sesame oil and 2 teaspoons of water. Heat a frying pan over a medium-high heat and swirl in 2 tablespoons of the egg mixture to form a paper-thin omelette. Remove and reserve. Repeat this process until all the egg has been used. Cook the rice in lightly salted boiling water for 12 minutes, or until tender. Drain and reserve.

Heat a wok, then add the remaining sesame oil with the groundnut oil and stir-fry the chicken for 5 minutes until cooked through. Using a slotted spoon, remove from the wok and keep warm.

Add the spring onions, carrot and sugar snap peas to the wok and stir-fry for 2–3 minutes. Add the prawns and stir-fry for 2–3 minutes, or until pink. Return the chicken to the wok with the Chinese five-spice powder and stir-fry for 1 minute. Stir in the drained rice.

Mix together the soy sauce, fish sauce and vinegar. Pour into the wok and continue to stir-fry for 2–3 minutes. Roll the papery omelettes into tight rolls and slice to form thin strips. Stir into the rice andserve immediately.

Try this: FOR AN ALTERNATIVE: 176   FOR ENTERTAINING: 130

Lemon Chicken Rice

SERVES 4

2 tbsp sunflower oil
4 chicken leg portions
1 medium onion,
    peeled and chopped
1–2 garlic cloves,
    peeled and crushed
1 tbsp curry powder

25 g/1 oz butter
225 g/8 oz long-grain
    white rice
1 lemon, preferably
    unwaxed, sliced
600 ml/1 pint chicken stock
salt and freshly ground

black pepper
2 tbsp flaked, toasted
    almonds
sprigs of fresh coriander,
    to garnish

Preheat the oven to 180°C/350°F/Gas Mark 4, about 10 minutes before required. Heat the oil in a large frying pan, add the chicken legs and cook, turning, until sealed and golden all over. Using a slotted spoon, remove from the pan and reserve.

Add the onion and garlic to the oil remaining in the frying pan and cook for 5–7 minutes, or until just beginning to brown. Sprinkle in the curry powder and cook, stirring, for a further 1 minute. Return the chicken to the pan and stir well, then remove from the heat.

Melt the butter in a large heavy-based saucepan. Add the rice and cook, stirring, to ensure that all the grains are coated in the melted butter, then remove from the heat.

Stir the lemon slices into the chicken mixture, then spoon the mixture onto the rice and pour over the stock. Season to taste with salt and pepper.

Cover with a tight-fitting lid and cook in the preheated oven for 45 minutes, or until the rice is tender and the chicken is cooked thoroughly. Serve sprinkled with the toasted flaked almonds and sprigs of coriander.

Try this: FOR AN ALTERNATIVE: 284   FOR ENTERTAINING: 270

Spiced Indian Roast Potatoes with Chicken

SERVES 4

700 g/1½ lb waxy potatoes, peeled and cut into large chunks
salt and freshly ground black pepper
4 tbsp sunflower oil
8 chicken drumsticks
1 large Spanish onion, peeled and roughly chopped
3 shallots, peeled and roughly chopped
2 large garlic cloves, peeled and crushed
1 red chilli
2 tsp fresh root ginger, peeled and finely grated
2 tsp ground cumin
2 tsp ground coriander
pinch of cayenne pepper
4 cardamom pods, crushed
sprigs of fresh coriander, to garnish

Preheat the oven to 190°C/375°F/Gas Mark 5, about 10 minutes before cooking. Parboil the potatoes for 5 minutes in lightly salted boiling water, then drain thoroughly and reserve. Heat the oil in a large frying pan, add the chicken drumsticks and cook until sealed on all sides. Remove and reserve.

Add the onions and shallots to the pan and fry for 4–5 minutes, or until softened. Stir in the garlic, chilli and ginger and cook for 1 minute, stirring constantly. Stir in the ground cumin, coriander, cayenne pepper and crushed cardamom pods and continue to cook, stirring, for a further minute.

Add the potatoes to the pan, then add the chicken. Season to taste with salt and pepper. Stir gently until the potatoes and chicken pieces are coated in the onion and spice mixture.

Spoon into a large roasting tin and roast in the preheated oven for 35 minutes, or until the chicken and potatoes are cooked thoroughly. Garnish with fresh coriander and serve immediately.

Try this: FOR AN ALTERNATIVE: 276   FOR ENTERTAINING: 318

Thai Stuffed Omelette

SERVES 4

1 shallot, peeled and
  roughly chopped
1 garlic clove, peeled and
  roughly chopped
1 small red chilli, deseeded
  and roughly chopped
15 g/½ oz coriander leaves
pinch of sugar
2 tsp light soy sauce
2 tsp Thai fish sauce
4 tbsp vegetable or

groundnut oil
175 g/6 oz skinless, boneless
  chicken breast, finely sliced
½ small aubergine, trimmed
  and diced
50 g/2 oz button or
  shiitake mushrooms,
  wiped and sliced
½ small red pepper,
  deseeded and sliced
50 g/2 oz fine green beans,

trimmed and halved
2 spring onions, trimmed
  and thickly sliced
25 g/1 oz peas, thawed
  if frozen
6 medium eggs
salt and freshly ground
  black pepper
sprig of fresh basil,
  to garnish

Place the shallot, garlic, chilli, coriander and sugar in the bowl of a spice grinder or food processor. Blend until finely chopped. Add the soy sauce, fish sauce and 1 tablespoon of the vegetable oil and blend briefly to mix into a paste. Reserve. Heat a wok or large frying pan, add 1 tablespoon of the oil and when hot, add the chicken and aubergine and stir-fry for 3–4 minutes, or until golden. Add the mushrooms, red pepper, green beans and spring onions and stir-fry for 3–4 minutes or until tender, adding the peas for the final 1 minute. Remove from the heat and stir in the reserved coriander paste. Reserve.

Beat the eggs in a bowl and season to taste with salt and pepper. Heat the remaining oil in a large, non-stick frying pan and add the eggs, tilting the pan so that the eggs cover the bottom. Stir the eggs until they are starting to set all over, then cook for 1–2 minutes, or until firm and set on the bottom but still slightly soft on top. Spoon the chicken and vegetable mixture on to one half of the omelette and carefully flip the other half over. Cook over a low heat for 2–3 minutes, or until the omelette is set and the chicken and vegetables are heated through. Garnish with a sprig of basil and serve immediately.

Try this: FOR AN ALTERNATIVE: 154   FOR ENTERTAINING: 78

Pad Thai

SERVES 4

225 g/8 oz flat rice noodles
2 tbsp vegetable oil
225 g/8 oz boneless
  chicken breast, skinned
  and thinly sliced
4 shallots, peeled and
  thinly sliced
2 garlic cloves, peeled and
  finely chopped
4 spring onions, trimmed
  and diagonally cut into

5 cm/2 inch pieces
350 g/12 oz fresh white crab
  meat or tiny prawns
75 g/3 oz fresh bean sprouts,
  rinsed and drained
2 tbsp preserved or fresh
  radish, chopped
2–3 tbsp roasted peanuts,
  chopped (optional)

For the sauce:
3 tbsp Thai fish sauce
  (nam pla)
2–3 tbsp rice vinegar or
  cider vinegar
1 tbsp chilli bean or
  oyster sauce
1 tbsp toasted sesame oil
1 tbsp light brown sugar
1 red chilli, deseeded and
  thinly sliced

To make the sauce, whisk all the sauce ingredients in a bowl and reserve. Put the rice noodles in a large bowl and pour over enough hot water to cover. Leave to stand for about 15 minutes until softened. Drain and rinse, then drain again.

Heat the oil in a wok over a high heat until hot, but not smoking. Add the chicken strips and stir-fry constantly until they begin to colour. Using a slotted spoon, transfer to a plate. Reduce the heat to medium-high. Add the shallots, garlic and spring onions and stir-fry for 1 minute. Stir in the rice noodles, then the reserved sauce; mix well.

Add the reserved chicken strips, with the crab meat or prawns, bean sprouts and radish and stir well. Cook for about 5 minutes, stirring frequently, until heated through. If the noodles begin to stick, add a little water.

Turn into a large shallow serving dish and sprinkle with the chopped peanuts, if desired. Serve immediately.

Try this: FOR AN ALTERNATIVE: 162   FOR ENTERTAINING: 366

Stir-fried Lemon Chicken

SERVES 4

350 g/12 oz boneless, skinless chicken breast
1 large egg white
5 tsp cornflour
3 tbsp vegetable or groundnut oil
150 ml/¼ pint chicken stock

2 tbsp fresh lemon juice
2 tbsp light soy sauce
1 tbsp Chinese rice wine or dry sherry
1 tbsp sugar
2 garlic cloves, peeled and finely chopped

¼ tsp dried chilli flakes, or to taste

To garnish:
lemon rind strips
red chilli slices

Using a sharp knife, trim the chicken, discarding any fat and cut into thin strips, about 5 cm/2 inch long and 1 cm/½ inch wide. Place in a shallow dish. Lightly whisk the egg white and 1 tablespoon of the cornflour together until smooth. Pour over the chicken strips and mix well until coated evenly. Leave to marinate in the refrigerator for at least 20 minutes.

When ready to cook, drain the chicken and reserve. Heat a wok or large frying pan, add the oil and when hot, add the chicken and stir-fry for 1–2 minutes, or until the chicken has turned white. Using a slotted spoon, remove from the wok and reserve.

Wipe the wok clean and return to the heat. Add the chicken stock, lemon juice, soy sauce, Chinese rice wine or sherry, sugar, garlic and chilli flakes and bring to the boil. Blend the remaining cornflour with 1 tablespoon of water and stir into the stock. Simmer for 1 minute.

Return the chicken to the wok and continue simmering for a further 2–3 minutes, or until the chicken is tender and the sauce has thickened. Garnish with lemon strips and red chilli slices. Serve immediately.

Try this: FOR AN ALTERNATIVE: 272 FOR ENTERTAINING: 296

Chinese Braised White Chicken with Three Sauces

SERVES 4

1.4 kg/3 lb oven-ready chicken
salt
6 spring onions, trimmed
5 cm/2 inch piece fresh root
  ginger, peeled and sliced
2 tsp Szechuan peppercorns,
  crushed
2½ tsp sea salt flakes or
  crushed coarse sea salt

2 tsp freshly grated
  root ginger
4 tbsp dark soy sauce
4 tbsp sunflower oil
1 tsp caster sugar
2 garlic cloves, finely chopped
3 tbsp light soy sauce
1 tbsp Chinese rice wine
  or dry sherry

1 tsp sesame oil
3 tbsp rice vinegar
1 small hot red chilli,
  deseeded and finely
  sliced spring onion
  curls, to garnish
freshly steamed
  saffron-flavoured rice,
  to serve

Remove any fat from inside the chicken, rub inside and out with ½ teaspoon of salt and leave for 20 minutes. Place 3.4 litres/6 pints water with 2 spring onions and the ginger in a saucepan and bring to the boil. Add the chicken, breast-side down, return to the boil, cover and simmer for 20 minutes. Remove from the heat and leave for 1 hour. Remove the chicken and leave to cool.

Dry-fry the Szechuan peppercorns in a nonstick frying pan until they darken slightly and smell aromatic. Crush, mix with the sea salt and reserve. Squeeze the juice from half of the grated ginger, mix with the dark soy sauce, 1 tablespoon of the sunflower oil and half the sugar. Reserve. Finely chop the remaining spring onions and mix with the remaining ginger and garlic in a bowl. Heat the remaining oil to smoking and pour over the onion and ginger. When they stop sizzling, stir in the light soy sauce, Chinese rice wine or sherry and sesame oil. Reserve.

Mix together the rice vinegar, remaining sugar and chilli. Stir until the sugar dissolves. Reserve. Remove the skin from the chicken, then remove the legs and cut them in two at the joint. Lift the breast meat away from the carcass in two pieces and slice thickly crossways. Sprinkle the pepper and salt mixture over the chicken, garnish with spring onion curls and serve with the dipping sauces, spring onion mixture and rice.

Try this: FOR AN ALTERNATIVE: 258   FOR ENTERTAINING: 282

Orange Roasted Whole Chicken

SERVES 6

1 small orange, thinly sliced
50 g/2 oz sugar
1.4 kg/3 lb oven-ready
  chicken
1 small bunch
  fresh coriander

1 small bunch fresh mint
2 tbsp olive oil
1 tsp Chinese five
  spice powder
½ tsp paprika
1 tsp fennel seeds, crushed

salt and freshly ground
  black pepper
sprigs of fresh coriander,
  to garnish
freshly cooked vegetables,
  to serve

Preheat the oven to 190°C/375°F/Gas Mark 5, 10 minutes before cooking. Place the orange slices in a small saucepan, cover with water, bring to the boil, then simmer for 2 minutes and drain. Place the sugar in a clean saucepan with 150 ml/¼ pint fresh water. Stir over a low heat until the sugar dissolves, then bring to the boil, add the drained orange slices and simmer for 10 minutes. Remove from the heat and leave in the syrup until cold.

Remove any excess fat from inside the chicken. Starting at the neck end, carefully loosen the skin of the chicken over the breast and legs without tearing. Push the orange slices under the loosened skin with the coriander and mint.

Mix together the olive oil, Chinese five spice powder, paprika and crushed fennel seeds and season to taste with salt and pepper. Brush the chicken skin generously with this mixture. Transfer to a wire rack set over a roasting tin and roast in the preheated oven for 1½ hours, or until the juices run clear when a skewer is inserted into the thickest part of the thigh. Remove from the oven and leave to rest for 10 minutes. Garnish with sprigs of fresh coriander and serve with freshly cooked vegetables.

Try this: FOR AN ALTERNATIVE: 278   FOR ENTERTAINING: 266

Baked Thai Chicken Wings

SERVES 4

4 tbsp clear honey
1 tbsp chilli sauce
1 garlic clove,
   peeled and crushed
1 tsp freshly grated
   root ginger
1 lemon grass stalk, outer
   leaves discarded and

finely chopped
2 tbsp lime zest
3–4 tbsp freshly squeezed
   lime juice
1 tbsp light soy sauce
1 tsp ground cumin
1 tsp ground coriander
¼ tsp ground cinnamon

1.4 kg/3 lb chicken wings
   (about 12 large wings)
6 tbsp mayonnaise
2 tbsp freshly
   chopped coriander
lemon or lime wedges,
   to garnish

Preheat the oven to 190°C/375°F/Gas Mark 5, 10 minutes before cooking. In a small saucepan, mix together the honey, chilli sauce, garlic, ginger, lemon grass, 1 tablespoon of the lime zest and 2 tablespoons of the lime juice with the soy sauce, cumin, coriander and cinnamon. Heat gently until just starting to bubble, then remove from the heat and leave to cool.

Prepare the chicken wings by folding the tips back under the thickest part of the meat to form a triangle. Arrange in a shallow, ovenproof dish. Pour over the honey mixture, turning the wings to ensure that they are all well coated. Cover with clingfilm and leave to marinate in the refrigerator for 4 hours or overnight, turning once or twice.

Mix together the mayonnaise with the remaining lime zest and juice and the coriander. Leave to let the flavours develop while the wings are cooking. Arrange the wings on a rack set over a tinfoil-lined roasting tin. Roast at the top of the preheated oven for 50–60 minutes, or until the wings are tender and golden, basting once or twice with the remaining marinade and turning once. Remove from the oven. Garnish the wings with lemon or lime wedges and serve immediately with the mayonnaise.

Thai Chicken with Chilli & Peanuts

SERVES 4

2 tbsp vegetable or groundnut oil
1 garlic clove, peeled and finely chopped
1 tsp dried chilli flakes
350 g/12 oz boneless, skinless chicken breast, finely sliced
1 tbsp Thai fish sauce
2 tbsp peanuts, roasted and roughly chopped
225 g/ 8 oz sugar snap peas
3 tbsp chicken stock
1 tbsp light soy sauce
1 tbsp dark soy sauce
large pinch of sugar
freshly chopped coriander, to garnish
boiled or steamed rice, to serve

Heat a wok or large frying pan, add the oil and when hot, carefully swirl the oil around the wok until the sides are lightly coated with the oil. Add the garlic and stir-fry for 10–20 seconds, or until starting to brown. Add the chilli flakes and stir-fry for a few seconds more.

Add the finely sliced chicken to the wok and stir-fry for 2–3 minutes, or until the chicken has turned white.

Add the following ingredients, stirring well after each addition: fish sauce, peanuts, sugar snap peas, chicken stock, light and dark soy sauces and sugar. Give a final stir.

Bring the contents of the wok to the boil, then simmer gently for 3–4 minutes, or until the chicken and vegetables are tender. Remove from the heat and tip into a warmed serving dish. Garnish with chopped coriander and serve immediately with boiled or steamed rice.

Try this: FOR AN ALTERNATIVE: 72   FOR ENTERTAINING: 166

Chicken in Black Bean Sauce

SERVES 4

450 g/1 lb skinless, boneless chicken breast fillets, cut into strips
1 tbsp light soy sauce
2 tbsp Chinese rice wine or dry sherry
salt
1 tsp caster sugar
1 tsp sesame oil
2 tsp cornflour

2 tbsp sunflower oil
2 green peppers, deseeded and diced
1 tbsp freshly grated root ginger
2 garlic cloves, peeled and roughly chopped
2 shallots, peeled and finely chopped
4 spring onions, trimmed

and finely sliced
3 tbsp salted black beans, chopped
150 ml/¼ pint chicken stock
shredded spring onions, to garnish
freshly cooked egg noodles, to serve

Place the chicken strips in a large bowl. Mix together the soy sauce, Chinese rice wine or sherry, a little salt, caster sugar, sesame oil and cornflour and pour over the chicken.

Heat the wok over a high heat, add the oil and when very hot, add the chicken strips and stir-fry for 2 minutes. Add the green peppers and stir-fry for a further 2 minutes. Then add the ginger, garlic, shallots, spring onions and black beans and continue to stir-fry for another 2 minutes.

Add 4 tablespoons of the stock, stir-fry for 1 minute, then pour in the remaining stock and bring to the boil. Reduce the heat and simmer the sauce for 3–4 minutes, or until the chicken is cooked and the sauce has thickened slightly. Garnish with the shredded spring onions and serve immediately with noodles.

Try this: FOR AN ALTERNATIVE: 210 FOR ENTERTAINING: 198

Thai Chicken Fried Rice

SERVES 4

175 g/6 oz boneless
   chicken breast
2 tbsp vegetable oil
2 garlic cloves, peeled and
   finely chopped
2 tsp medium curry paste

450 g/1 lb cold cooked rice
1 tbsp light soy sauce
2 tbsp Thai fish sauce
large pinch of sugar
freshly ground black pepper

To garnish:
2 spring onions, trimmed
   and shredded lengthways
½ small onion, peeled and
   very finely sliced

Using a sharp knife, trim the chicken, discarding any sinew or fat and cut into small cubes. Reserve.

Heat a wok or large frying pan, add the oil and when hot, add the garlic and cook for 10–20 seconds or until just golden. Add the curry paste and stir-fry for a few seconds. Add the chicken and stir-fry for 3–4 minutes, or until tender and the chicken has turned white.

Stir the cold cooked rice into the chicken mixture, then add the soy sauce, fish sauce and sugar, stirring well after each addition. Stir-fry for 2–3 minutes, or until the chicken is cooked through and the rice is piping hot.

Check the seasoning and, if necessary, add a little extra soy sauce. Turn the rice and chicken mixture into a warmed serving dish. Season lightly with black pepper and garnish with shredded spring onion and onion slices. Serve immediately.

 Try this: FOR AN ALTERNATIVE: 262   FOR ENTERTAINING: 264

Chicken Chow Mein

SERVES 4

225 g/8 oz egg noodles
5 tsp sesame oil
4 tsp light soy sauce
2 tbsp Chinese rice wine
   or dry sherry
salt and freshly ground
   black pepper
225 g/8 oz skinless chicken

breast fillets, cut into strips
3 tbsp groundnut oil
2 garlic cloves, peeled and
   finely chopped
50 g/2 oz mangetout peas,
   finely sliced
50 g/2 oz cooked ham, cut
   into fine strips

2 tsp dark soy sauce
pinch of sugar

To garnish:
shredded spring onions
toasted sesame seeds

Bring a large saucepan of water to the boil and add the noodles. Cook for 3–5 minutes, drain and plunge into cold water. Drain again, add 1 tablespoon of the sesame oil and stir lightly.

Place 2 teaspoons of light soy sauce, 1 tablespoon of Chinese rice wine or sherry, and 1 teaspoon of the sesame oil, with seasoning to taste in a bowl. Add the chicken and stir well. Cover lightly and leave to marinate in the refrigerator for about 15 minutes.

Heat the wok over a high heat, add 1 tablespoon of the groundnut oil and when very hot, add the chicken and its marinade and stir-fry for 2 minutes. Remove the chicken and juices and reserve. Wipe the wok clean with absorbent kitchen paper.

Reheat the wok and add the oil. Add the garlic and toss in the oil for 20 seconds. Add the mangetout peas and the ham and stir-fry for 1 minute. Add the noodles, remaining light soy sauce, Chinese rice wine or sherry, the dark soy sauce and sugar. Season to taste with salt and pepper and stir-fry for 2 minutes. Add the chicken and juices to the wok and stir-fry for 4 minutes, or until the chicken is cooked. Drizzle over the remaining sesame oil. Garnish with spring onions and sesame seeds and serve.

Try this: FOR AN ALTERNATIVE: 174 FOR ENTERTAINING: 258

Chicken Satay Salad

SERVES 4

4 tbsp crunchy peanut butter
1 tbsp chilli sauce
1 garlic clove, peeled
   and crushed
2 tbsp cider vinegar
2 tbsp light soy sauce
2 tbsp dark soy sauce

2 tsp soft brown sugar
pinch of salt
2 tsp freshly ground
   Szechuan peppercorns
450 g/1 lb dried egg noodles
2 tbsp sesame oil
1 tbsp groundnut oil

450 g/1 lb skinless, boneless
   chicken breast fillets, cut
   into cubes
shredded celery leaves,
   to garnish
cos lettuce, to serve

Place the peanut butter, chilli sauce, garlic, cider vinegar, soy sauces, sugar, salt and ground peppercorns in a food processor and blend to form a smooth paste. Scrape into a bowl, cover and chill in the refrigerator until required.

Bring a large saucepan of lightly salted water to the boil. Add the noodles and cook for 3–5 minutes. Drain and plunge into cold water. Drain again and toss in the sesame oil. Leave to cool.

Heat the wok until very hot, add the oil and when hot, add the chicken cubes. Stir-fry for 5–6 minutes until the chicken is golden brown and cooked through.

Remove the chicken from the wok using a slotted spoon and add to the noodles, together with the peanut sauce. Mix lightly together, then sprinkle with the shredded celery leaves and either serve immediately or leave until cold, then serve with cos lettuce.

Try this: FOR AN ALTERNATIVE: 254   FOR ENTERTAINING: 152

Chicken & Baby Vegetable Stir Fry

SERVES 4

2 tbsp groundnut oil
1 small red chilli, deseeded and finely chopped
150 g/5 oz chicken breast or thigh meat, skinned and cut into cubes
2 baby leeks, trimmed and sliced
12 asparagus spears, halved

125 g/4 oz mangetout peas, trimmed
125 g/4 oz baby carrots, trimmed and halved lengthways
125 g/4 oz fine green beans, trimmed and diagonally sliced
125 g/4 oz baby sweetcorn,

diagonally halved
50 ml/2 fl oz chicken stock
2 tsp light soy sauce
1 tbsp dry sherry
1 tsp sesame oil
toasted sesame seeds, to garnish

Heat the wok until very hot and add the oil. Add the chopped chilli and chicken and stir-fry for 4–5 minutes, or until the chicken is cooked and golden.

Increase the heat, add the leeks to the chicken and stir-fry for 2 minutes. Add the asparagus spears, mangetout peas, baby carrots, green beans, and baby sweetcorn. Stir-fry for 3–4 minutes, or until the vegetables soften slightly but still retain a slight crispness.

In a small bowl, mix together the chicken stock, soy sauce, dry sherry and sesame oil. Pour into the wok, stir and cook until heated through. Sprinkle with the toasted sesame seeds and serve immediately.

Try this: FOR AN ALTERNATIVE: 168   FOR ENTERTAINING: 374

Thai Coconut Chicken

SERVES 4

1 tsp cumin seeds
1 tsp mustard seeds
1 tsp coriander seeds
1 tsp turmeric
1 bird's-eye chilli, deseeded
and finely chopped
1 tbsp freshly grated
root ginger

2 garlic cloves, peeled and
finely chopped
125 ml/4 fl oz double cream
8 skinless chicken thighs
2 tbsp groundnut oil
1 onion, peeled and
finely sliced
200 ml/7 fl oz coconut milk

salt and freshly ground
black pepper
4 tbsp freshly
chopped coriander
2 spring onions,
shredded, to garnish
freshly cooked Thai fragrant
rice, to serve

Heat the wok and add the cumin seeds, mustard seeds and coriander seeds. Dry-fry over a low to medium heat for 2 minutes, or until the fragrance becomes stronger and the seeds start to pop. Add the turmeric and leave to cool slightly. Grind the spices in a pestle and mortar or blend to a fine powder in a food processor.

Mix the chilli, ginger, garlic and the cream together in a small bowl, add the ground spices and mix. Place the chicken thighs in a shallow dish and spread the spice paste over the thighs.

Heat the wok over a high heat, add the oil and when hot, add the onion and stir-fry until golden brown. Add the chicken and spice paste. Cook for 5–6 minutes, stirring occasionally, until evenly coloured. Add the coconut milk and season to taste with salt and pepper.

Simmer the chicken for 15–20 minutes, or until the thighs are cooked through, taking care not to allow the mixture to boil. Stir in the chopped coriander and serve immediately with the freshly cooked rice sprinkled with shredded spring onions.

Try this: FOR AN ALTERNATIVE: 164   FOR ENTERTAINING: 18

Stir–fried Chicken with Basil

SERVES 4

3 tbsp sunflower oil
3 tbsp green curry paste
450 g/1 lb skinless,
   boneless chicken breast
   fillets, trimmed and cut
   into cubes
8 cherry tomatoes

100 ml/4 fl oz coconut cream
2 tbsp soft brown sugar
2 tbsp Thai fish sauce
1 red chilli, deseeded and
   thinly sliced
1 green chilli, deseeded
   and thinly sliced

75 g/3 oz fresh torn
   basil leaves
sprigs of fresh coriander,
   to garnish
freshly steamed white rice,
   to serve

Heat the wok, then add the oil and heat for 1 minute. Add the green curry paste and cook, stirring for 1 minute to release the flavour and cook the paste. Add the chicken and stir-fry over a high heat for 2 minutes, making sure the chicken is coated thoroughly with the green curry paste.

Reduce the heat under the wok, then add the cherry tomatoes and cook, stirring gently, for 2–3 minutes, or until the tomatoes burst and begin to disintegrate into the green curry paste.

Add half the coconut cream and add to the wok with the brown sugar, Thai fish sauce and the red and green chillies. Stir-fry gently for 5 minutes, or until the sauce is amalgamated and the chicken is cooked thoroughly.

Just before serving, sprinkle the chicken with the torn basil leaves and add the remaining coconut cream, then serve immediately with freshly steamed white rice garnished with fresh coriander sprigs.

Try this: FOR AN ALTERNATIVE: 314   FOR ENTERTAINING: 330

Steamed, Crispy, Citrus Chicken

SERVES 6

200 ml/7 fl oz light soy sauce
1 tbsp brown sugar
4 star anise
2 slices fresh root
   ginger, peeled
5 spring onions, trimmed
   and sliced

1 small orange,
   cut into wedges
1 lime, cut into wedges
1.1 kg/2 ½ lb chicken
2 garlic cloves, peeled and
   finely chopped
2 tbsp Chinese rice wine

2 tbsp dark soy sauce
300 ml/½ pint groundnut oil
orange slices, to garnish
freshly cooked steamed rice,
   to serve

Pour the light soy sauce and 200 ml/7 fl oz water into the wok and add the sugar and star anise. Bring to the boil over a gentle heat. Pour into a small bowl and leave to cool slightly. Wipe the wok clean with absorbent kitchen paper.

Put the ginger, 2 spring onions, orange and lime inside the cavity of the chicken. Place a rack in the wok and pour in boiling water to a depth of 5 cm/2 inches. Put a piece of tinfoil onto the rack and place the chicken in the centre, then pour over the soy sauce mixture.

Cover the wok and steam gently for 1–1 hour 10 minutes, or until the chicken is cooked through, pouring off excess fat from time to time. Add more water if necessary. Leave the chicken to cool and dry for up to 3 hours, then cut the chicken into quarters.

Mix together the garlic, Chinese rice wine, dark soy sauce and remaining spring onions, then reserve. Dry the wok and heat again, then add the oil. When hot, shallow fry the chicken quarters for 4 minutes, or until golden and crisp. Do this one portion at a time, remove and drain on absorbent kitchen paper.

When cool enough to handle, shred into bite-sized pieces and drizzle over the sauce. Garnish with slices of orange and serve with freshly steamed rice.

Try this: FOR AN ALTERNATIVE: 336   FOR ENTERTAINING: 326

Chicken & Cashew Nuts

SERVES 4

450 g/1 lb skinless chicken,
  boneless breast fillets, cut
  into 1 cm/½ inch cubes
1 medium egg white, beaten
1 tsp salt
1 tsp sesame oil
2 tsp cornflour

300 ml/½ pint groundnut oil
  for deep frying
2 tsp sunflower oil
50 g/2 oz unsalted cashews
4 spring onions, shredded
50 g/2 oz mangetout peas,
  diagonally sliced

1 tbsp Chinese rice wine
1 tbsp light soy sauce
shredded spring onions,
  to garnish
freshly steamed white rice
  with fresh coriander
  leaves, to serve

Place the cubes of chicken in a large bowl. Add the egg white, salt, sesame oil and cornflour. Mix well to ensure the chicken is coated thoroughly. Chill in the refrigerator for 20 minutes.

Heat the wok until very hot, add the groundnut oil and when hot, remove the wok from the heat and add the chicken. Stir continuously to prevent the chicken from sticking to the wok. When the chicken turns white, after about 2 minutes, remove it using a slotted spoon and reserve. Discard the oil.

Wipe the wok clean with absorbent kitchen paper and heat it again until very hot. Add the sunflower oil and heat. When hot, add the cashew nuts, spring onions and mangetout peas and stir-fry for 1 minute.

Add the rice wine and soy sauce. Return the chicken to the wok and stir-fry for 2 minutes. Garnish with shredded spring onions and serve immediately with freshly steamed rice sprinkled with fresh coriander.

Try this: FOR AN ALTERNATIVE: 280   FOR ENTERTAINING: 212

Chinese–glazed Poussin with Green & Black Rice

SERVES 4

4 oven-ready poussins
salt and freshly ground
  black pepper
300 ml/½ pint apple juice
1 cinnamon stick
2 star anise
½ tsp Chinese five
  spice powder

50 g/2 oz dark
  muscovado sugar
2 tbsp tomato ketchup
1 tbsp cider vinegar
grated rind of 1 orange
350 g/12 oz mixed basmati
  white and wild rice
125 g/4 oz mangetout, finely

sliced lengthways
1 bunch spring onions,
  trimmed and finely
  shredded lengthways
salt and freshly ground
  black pepper

Preheat the oven to 200°C/400°F/Gas Mark 6, 15 minutes before cooking. Rinse the poussins inside and out and pat dry with absorbent kitchen paper. Using tweezers, remove any feathers. Season well with salt and pepper, then reserve. Pour the apple juice into a small saucepan and add the cinnamon stick, star anise and Chinese five spice powder. Bring to the boil, then simmer rapidly until reduced by half. Reduce the heat, stir in the sugar, tomato ketchup, vinegar and orange rind and simmer gently until the sugar is dissolved and the glaze is syrupy. Remove from the heat and leave to cool completely. Remove the whole spices.

Place the poussins on a wire rack set over a tinfoil-lined roasting tin. Brush generously with the apple glaze. Roast in the preheated oven for 40–45 minutes, or until the juices run clear when the thigh is pierced with a skewer, basting once or twice with the remaining glaze. Remove the poussins from the oven and leave to cool slightly.

Meanwhile, cook the rice according to the packet instructions. Bring a large saucepan of lightly salted water to the boil and add the mangetout. Blanch for 1 minute, then drain thoroughly. As soon as the rice is cooked, drain and transfer to a warmed bowl. Add the mangetout and spring onions, season to taste and stir well. Arrange on warmed dinner plates, place a poussin on top and serve immediately.

Try this: FOR AN ALTERNATIVE: 318 FOR ENTERTAINING: 276

Teriyaki Turkey with Oriental Vegetables

SERVES 4

1 red chilli
1 garlic clove, peeled
  and crushed
2.5 cm/1 inch piece root
  ginger, peeled and grated
3 tbsp dark soy sauce
1 tsp sunflower oil
350 g/12 oz skinless,

boneless turkey breast
1 tbsp sesame oil
1 tbsp sesame seeds
2 carrots, peeled and cut
  into matchstick strips
1 leek, trimmed and shredded
125 g/4 oz broccoli, cut into
  tiny florets

1 tsp cornflour
3 tbsp dry sherry
125 g/4 oz mangetout,
  cut into thin strips

To serve:
freshly cooked egg noodles
sprinkling of sesame seeds

Halve, deseed and thinly slice the chilli. Put into a small bowl with the garlic, ginger, soy sauce and sunflower oil. Cut the turkey into thin strips. Add to the mixture and mix until well coated. Cover with clingfilm and marinate in the refrigerator for at least 30 minutes.

Heat a wok or large frying pan. Add 2 teaspoons of the sesame oil. When hot, remove the turkey from the marinade. Stir-fry for 2–3 minutes until browned and cooked. Remove from the pan and reserve.

Heat the remaining 1 teaspoon of oil in the wok. Add the sesame seeds and stir-fry for a few seconds until they start to change colour. Add the carrots, leek and broccoli and continue stir-frying for 2–3 minutes.

Blend the cornflour with 1 tablespoon of cold water to make a smooth paste. Stir in the sherry and marinade. Add to the wok with the mangetout and cook for 1 minute, stirring all the time until thickened. Return the turkey to the pan and continue cooking for 1–2 minutes or until the turkey is hot, the vegetables are tender and the sauce is bubbling. Serve the turkey and vegetables immediately with the egg noodles. Sprinkle with the sesame seeds.

Try this: FOR AN ALTERNATIVE: 158 FOR ENTERTAINING: 74

Turkey with Oriental Mushrooms

SERVES 4

15 g/½ oz dried
  Chinese mushrooms
450 g/1 lb turkey
  breast steaks
150 ml/¼ pint turkey
  or chicken stock
2 tbsp groundnut oil
1 red pepper, deseeded

and sliced
225 g/8 oz sugar snap peas,
  trimmed
125 g/4 oz shiitake
  mushrooms, wiped
  and halved
125 g/4 oz oyster
  mushrooms, wiped

and halved
2 tbsp yellow bean sauce
2 tbsp soy sauce
1 tbsp hot chilli sauce
freshly cooked noodles,
  to serve

Place the dried mushrooms in a small bowl, cover with almost boiling water and leave for 20–30 minutes. Drain and discard any woody stems from the mushrooms. Cut the turkey and into thin strips.

Pour the turkey or chicken stock into a wok or large frying pan and bring to the boil. Add the turkey and cook gently for 3 minutes, or until the turkey is sealed completely, then using a slotted spoon, remove from the wok and reserve. Discard any stock.

Wipe the wok clean and reheat, then add the oil. When the oil is almost smoking, add the drained turkey and stir-fry for 2 minutes. Add the drained mushrooms to the wok with the red pepper, the sugar snap peas and the shiitake and oyster mushrooms. Stir-fry for 2 minutes, then add the yellow bean, soy and hot chilli sauces.

Stir-fry the mixture for 1–2 minutes more, or until the turkey is cooked thoroughly and the vegetables are cooked but still retain a bite. Turn into a warmed serving dish and serve immediately with freshly cooked noodles.

Try this: FOR AN ALTERNATIVE: 366   FOR ENTERTAINING: 346

Turkey & Vegetable Stir Fry

SERVES 4

350 g/12 oz mixed vegetables, such as baby sweetcorn, 1 small red pepper, pak choi, mushrooms, broccoli florets and baby carrots
1 red chilli
2 tbsp groundnut oil
350 g/12 oz skinless, boneless turkey breast, sliced into fine strips across the grain

2 garlic cloves, peeled and finely chopped
2.5 cm/1 inch piece fresh root ginger, peeled and finely grated
3 spring onions, trimmed and finely sliced
2 tbsp light soy sauce
1 tbsp Chinese rice wine or dry sherry
2 tbsp chicken stock or water
1 tsp cornflour

1 tsp sesame oil
freshly cooked noodles or rice, to serve

To garnish:
50 g/2 oz toasted cashew nuts
2 spring onions, finely shredded
25 g/1 oz beansprouts

Slice or chop the vegetables into small pieces, depending on which you use. Halve the baby sweetcorn lengthways, deseed and thinly slice the red pepper, tear or shred the pak choi, slice the mushrooms, break the broccoli into small florets and cut the carrots into matchsticks. Deseed and finely chop the chilli.

Heat a wok or large frying pan, add the oil and when hot, add the turkey strips and stir-fry for 1 minute or until they turn white. Add the garlic, ginger, spring onions and chilli and cook for a few seconds. Add the prepared carrot, pepper, broccoli and mushrooms and stir-fry for 1 minute. Add the baby sweetcorn and pak choi and stir-fry for 1 minute.

Blend the soy sauce, Chinese rice wine or sherry and stock or water and pour over the vegetables. Blend the cornflour with 1 teaspoon of water and stir into the vegetables, mixing well. Bring to the boil, reduce the heat, then simmer for 1 minute. Stir in the sesame oil. Tip into a warmed serving dish, sprinkle with cashew nuts, shredded spring onions and beansprouts. Serve immediately with noodles or rice.

Try this: FOR AN ALTERNATIVE: 290   FOR ENTERTAINING: 352

Thai Stir-fried Spicy Turkey

SERVES 4

2 tbsp Thai fragrant rice
2 tbsp lemon juice
3–5 tbsp chicken stock
2 tbsp Thai fish sauce
½–1 tsp cayenne pepper,
    or to taste

125 g/4 oz fresh turkey mince
2 shallots, peeled and
    chopped
½ lemon grass stalk, outer
    leaves discarded and
    finely sliced

1 lime leaf, finely sliced
1 spring onion, trimmed
    and finely chopped
freshly chopped coriander,
    to garnish
Chinese leaves,to serve

Place the rice in a small frying pan and cook, stirring constantly, over a medium high heat for 4–5 minutes, or until the rice is browned. Transfer to a spice grinder or blender and pulse briefly until roughly ground. Reserve.

Place the lemon juice, 3 tablespoons of the stock, the fish sauce and cayenne pepper into a small saucepan and bring to the boil. Add the turkey mince and return to the boil. Continue cooking over a high heat until the turkey is sealed all over.

Add the shallots to the saucepan with the lemon grass, lime leaf, spring onion and reserved rice. Continue cooking for another 1–2 minutes, or until the turkey is cooked through, adding a little more stock, if necessary to keep the mixture moist.

Spoon a little of the mixture into each Chinese leaf and arrange on a serving dish or individual plates. Garnish with a little chopped coriander and serve immediately.

Try this: FOR AN ALTERNATIVE: 244   FOR ENTERTAINING: 350

Szechuan Turkey Noodles

SERVES 4

1 tbsp tomato paste
2 tsp black bean sauce
2 tsp cider vinegar
salt and freshly ground
  black pepper
½ tsp Szechuan pepper
2 tsp sugar
4 tsp sesame oil

225 g/8 oz dried egg noodles
2 tbsp groundnut oil
2 tsp freshly grated
  root ginger
3 garlic cloves, peeled
  and roughly chopped
2 shallots, peeled and
  finely chopped

2 courgettes, trimmed and
  cut into fine matchsticks
450 g/1 lb turkey breast,
  skinned and cut into strips
deep-fried onion rings,
  to garnish

Mix together the tomato paste, black bean sauce, cider vinegar, a pinch of salt and pepper, the sugar and half the sesame oil. Chill in the refrigerator for 30 minutes.

Bring a large saucepan of lightly salted water to the boil and add the noodles. Cook for 3–5 minutes, drain and plunge immediately into cold water. Toss with the remaining sesame oil and reserve.

Heat the wok until very hot, then add the oil and when hot, add the ginger, garlic and shallots. Stir-fry for 20 seconds, then add the courgettes and turkey strips. Stir-fry for 3–4 minutes, or until the turkey strips are sealed.

Add the prepared chilled black bean sauce and continue to stir-fry for another 4 minutes over a high heat. Add the drained noodles to the wok and stir until the noodles, turkey, vegetables and the sauce are well mixed together. Garnish with the deep-fried onion rings and serve immediately.

Try this: FOR AN ALTERNATIVE: 306   FOR ENTERTAINING: 294

Sweet & Sour Turkey

SERVES 4

2 tbsp groundnut oil
2 garlic cloves, peeled
   and chopped
1 tbsp freshly grated
   root ginger
4 spring onions, trimmed
   and cut into 4 cm/1½ inch
   lengths

450 g/1 lb turkey breast,
   skinned and cut into strips
1 red pepper, deseeded and
   cut into 2.5 cm/1 inch
   squares
225 g/8 oz canned water
   chestnuts, drained
150 ml/¼ pint chicken stock

2 tbsp Chinese rice wine
3 tbsp light soy sauce
2 tsp dark soy sauce
2 tbsp tomato paste
2 tbsp white wine vinegar
1 tbsp sugar
1 tbsp cornflour
egg fried rice, to serve

Heat the wok over a high heat, add the oil and when hot, add the garlic, ginger and spring onions, stir-fry for 20 seconds.

Add the turkey to the wok and stir-fry for 2 minutes, or until beginning to colour. Add the peppers and water chestnuts and stir-fry for a further 2 minutes.

Mix the chicken stock, Chinese rice wine, light and dark soy sauce, tomato paste, white wine vinegar and the sugar together in a small jug or bowl. Add the mixture to the wok, stir and bring the sauce to the boil.

Mix together the cornflour with 2 tablespoons of water and add to the wok. Reduce the heat and simmer for 3 minutes, or until the turkey is cooked thoroughly and the sauce slightly thickened and glossy. Serve immediately with egg fried rice.

Try this: FOR AN ALTERNATIVE: 102   FOR ENTERTAINING: 202

Noodles with Turkey & Mushrooms

SERVES 4

225 g/8 oz dried egg noodles
1 tbsp groundnut oil
1 red onion, peeled and sliced
2 tbsp freshly grated
    root ginger
3 garlic cloves, peeled and

finely chopped
350 g/12 oz turkey breast,
    skinned and cut into strips
125 g/4 oz baby button
    mushrooms
150 g/5 oz chestnut

mushrooms
2 tbsp dark soy sauce
2 tbsp hoisin sauce
2 tbsp dry sherry
4 tbsp vegetable stock
2 tsp cornflour

Bring a large saucepan of lightly salted water to the boil and add the noodles. Cook for 3–5 minutes, then drain and plunge immediately into cold water. When cool, drain again and reserve.

Heat the wok, add the oil and when hot, add the onion and stir-fry for 3 minutes until it starts to soften. Add the ginger and garlic and stir-fry for a further 3 minutes, then add the turkey strips and stir-fry for 4–5 minutes until sealed and golden.

Wipe and slice the chestnut mushrooms into similar-sized pieces and add to the wok with the whole button mushrooms. Stir-fry for 3–4 minutes, or until tender. When all the vegetables are tender and the turkey is cooked, add the soy sauce, hoisin sauce, sherry and vegetable stock.

Mix the cornflour with 2 tablespoons of water and add to the wok, then cook, stirring, until the sauce thickens. Add the drained noodles to the wok, then toss the mixture together and serve immediately.

Try this: FOR AN ALTERNATIVE: 304   FOR ENTERTAINING: 44

Lime & Sesame Turkey

SERVES 4

450 g/1 lb turkey breast, skinned and cut into strips
2 lemon grass stalks, outer leaves discarded and finely sliced
grated zest of 1 lime
4 garlic cloves, peeled and crushed

6 shallots, peeled and finely sliced
2 tbsp Thai fish sauce
2 tsp soft brown sugar
1 small red chilli, deseeded and finely sliced
3 tbsp sunflower oil
1 tbsp sesame oil

225 g/8 oz stir-fry rice noodles
1 tbsp sesame seeds
shredded spring onions, to garnish
freshly stir-fried vegetables, to serve

Place the turkey strips in a shallow dish. Mix together the lemon grass stalks, lime zest, garlic, shallots, Thai fish sauce, sugar and chilli with 2 tablespoons of the sunflower oil and the sesame oil. Pour over the turkey. Cover and leave to marinate in the refrigerator for 2–3 hours, spooning the marinade over the turkey occasionally.

Soak the noodles in warm water for 5 minutes. Drain through a sieve or colander, then plunge immediately into cold water. Drain again and reserve until ready to use.

Heat the wok until very hot and add the sesame seeds. Dry-fry for 1–2 minutes, or until toasted in colour. Remove from the wok and reserve. Wipe the wok to remove any dust left from the seeds:

Heat the wok again and add the remaining sunflower oil. When hot, drain the turkey from the marinade and stir-fry for 3–4 minutes, or until golden brown and cooked through (you may need to do this in two batches). When all the turkey has been cooked, add the noodles to the wok and cook, stirring, for 1–2 minutes, or until heated through thoroughly. Garnish with the shredded spring onions, toasted sesame seeds and serve immediately with freshly stir-fried vegetables of your choice.

Try this: FOR AN ALTERNATIVE: 296   FOR ENTERTAINING: 272

Crispy Aromatic Duck

SERVES 4-6

2 tbsp Chinese five
  spice powder
75 g/3 oz Szechuan
  peppercorns, lightly
  crushed
25 g/1 oz whole black
  peppercorns, lightly
  crushed
3 tbsp cumin seeds,
  lightly crushed

200 g/7 oz rock salt
2.7 kg/6 lb oven-ready duck
7.5 cm/3 inch piece fresh
  root ginger, peeled and
  cut into 6 slices
6 spring onions, trimmed
  and cut into 7.5 cm/3
  inch lengths
cornflour for dusting
1.1 litres/2 pints groundnut oil

To serve:
warm Chinese pancakes
spring onion, cut into shreds
cucumber, cut into slices
  lengthways
hoisin sauce

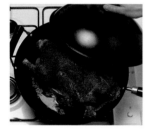

Mix together the Chinese five spice powder, Szechuan and black peppercorns, cumin seeds and salt. Rub the duck inside and out with the spice mixture. Wrap the duck with clingfilm and place in the refrigerator for 24 hours. Brush any loose spices from the duck. Place the ginger and spring onions into the duck cavity and put the duck on a heatproof plate.

Place a wire rack in a wok and pour in boiling water to a depth of 5 cm/2 inches. Lower the duck and plate on to the rack and cover. Steam gently for 2 hours or until the duck is cooked through, pouring off excess fat from time to time and adding more water, if necessary. Remove the duck, pour off all the liquid and discard the ginger and spring onions. Leave the duck in a cool place for 2 hours, or until it has dried and cooled.

Cut the duck into quarters and dust lightly with cornflour. Heat the oil in a wok or deep-fat fryer to 190°C/375°F, then deep-fry the duck quarters two at a time. Cook the breast for 8–10 minutes and the thighs and legs for 12–14 minutes, or until each piece is heated through. Drain on absorbent kitchen paper, then shred with a fork. Serve immediately with warm Chinese pancakes, spring onion shreds, cucumber slices and hoisin sauce.

Try this: FOR AN ALTERNATIVE: 326 FOR ENTERTAINING: 336

Hot & Sour Duck

SERVES 4

4 small boneless duck breasts, with skin on, thinly sliced on the diagonal	2.5 cm/1 inch piece fresh root ginger, chopped	227 g can bamboo shoots, drained, rinsed and finely sliced
1 tsp salt	1 tsp ground coriander	salt and freshly ground black pepper
4 tbsp tamarind pulp	3 large red chillies, deseeded and chopped	sprigs of fresh coriander, to garnish
4 shallots, peeled and chopped	½ tsp turmeric	freshly cooked rice, to serve
2 garlic cloves, peeled and chopped	6 blanched almonds, chopped	
	125 ml/4 fl oz vegetable oil	

Sprinkle the duck with the salt, cover lightly and refrigerate for 20 minutes.

Meanwhile, place the tamarind pulp in a small bowl, pour over 4 tablespoons of hot water and leave for 2–3 minutes or until softened. Press the mixture through a sieve into another bowl to produce about 2 tablespoons of smooth juice.

Place the tamarind juice in a food processor with the shallots, garlic, ginger, coriander, chillies, turmeric and almonds. Blend until smooth, adding a little more hot water if necessary, and reserve the paste.

Heat a wok or large frying pan, add the oil and when hot, stir-fry the duck in batches for about 3 minutes, or until just coloured, then drain on absorbent kitchen paper.

Discard all but 2 tablespoons of the oil in the wok. Return to the heat. Add the paste and stir-fry for 5 minutes. Add the duck and stir-fry for 2 minutes. Add the bamboo shoots and stir-fry for 2 minutes. Season to taste with salt and pepper. Turn into a warmed serving dish, garnish with a sprig of fresh coriander and serve immediately with rice.

Try this: FOR AN ALTERNATIVE: 246   FOR ENTERTAINING: 82

Fried Ginger Rice
with Soy Glazed Duck

SERVES 4-6

2 duck breasts, skinned and diagonally cut into thin slices
2–3 tbsp Japanese soy sauce
1 tbsp mirin (sweet rice wine) or sherry
2 tbsp brown sugar
5 cm/2 inch piece of fresh root ginger, peeled and finely chopped

4 tbsp peanut or vegetable oil
2 garlic cloves, peeled and crushed
300 g/11 oz long-grain brown rice
900 ml/1½ pints chicken stock
freshly ground black pepper
125 g/4 oz lean ham, diced
175 g/6 oz mangetout,

diagonally cut in half
8 spring onions, trimmed and diagonally thinly sliced
1 tbsp freshly chopped coriander
sweet or hot chilli sauce, to taste (optional)
sprigs of fresh coriander, to garnish

Put the duck slices in a bowl with 1 tablespoon of the soy sauce, the mirin, 1 teaspoon of the sugar and one third of the ginger; stir. Leave to stand. Heat 2 tablespoons of the oil in a large, heavy-based saucepan. Add the garlic and half the remaining ginger and stir-fry for 1 minute. Add the rice and cook for 3 minutes, stirring constantly, until translucent. Stir in all but 125 ml/4 fl oz of the stock, with 1 teaspoon of the soy sauce, and bring to the boil. Season with pepper. Reduce the heat to very low and simmer, covered, for 25–30 minutes until the rice is tender and the liquid is absorbed. Cover and leave to stand.

Heat the remaining oil in a large frying pan or wok. Drain the duck strips and add to the frying pan. Stir-fry for 2–3 minutes until just coloured. Add 1 tablespoon of soy sauce and the remaining sugar and cook for 1 minute until glazed. Transfer to a plate and keep warm.

Stir in the ham, mangetout, spring onions, the remaining ginger and the chopped coriander. Add the remaining stock and duck marinade and cook until the liquid is almost reduced. Fork in the rice and a little chilli sauce to taste (if using); stir well. Turn into a serving dish and top with the duck. Garnish with coriander sprigs and serve immediately.

Try this: FOR AN ALTERNATIVE: 334   FOR ENTERTAINING: 142

Duck in Black Bean Sauce

SERVES 4

450 g/1 lb duck breast, skinned	root ginger	vegetable oil
1 tbsp light soy sauce	3 garlic cloves	150 ml/¼ pint chicken stock
1 tbsp Chinese rice wine or dry sherry	2 spring onions	shredded spring onions, to garnish
2.5 cm/1 inch piece fresh	2 tbsp Chinese preserved black beans	freshly cooked noodles, to serve
	1 tbsp groundnut or	

Using a sharp knife, trim the duck breasts, removing any fat. Slice thickly and place in a shallow dish. Mix together the soy sauce and Chinese rice wine or sherry and pour over the duck. Leave to marinate for 1 hour in the refrigerator, then drain and discard the marinade.

Peel the ginger and chop finely. Peel the garlic cloves and either chop finely or crush. Trim the root from the spring onions, discard the outer leaves and chop. Finely chop the black beans.

Heat a wok or large frying pan, add the oil and when very hot, add the ginger, garlic, spring onions and black beans and stir-fry for 30 seconds. Add the drained duck and stir-fry for 3–5 minutes or until the duck is browned.

Add the chicken stock to the wok, bring to the boil, then reduce the heat and simmer for 5 minutes, or until the duck is cooked and the sauce is reduced and thickened. Remove from the heat. Tip on to a bed of freshly cooked noodles, garnish with spring onion shreds and serve immediately.

Try this: FOR AN ALTERNATIVE: 282   FOR ENTERTAINING: 210

Crispy Roast Duck Legs with Pancakes

SERVES 6

900 g/2 lb plums, halved
25 g/1 oz butter
2 star anise
1 tsp freshly grated
   root ginger
50 g/2 oz soft brown sugar

zest and juice of 1 orange
salt and freshly ground
   black pepper
4 duck legs
3 tbsp dark soy sauce
2 tbsp dark brown sugar

½ cucumber, cut into
   matchsticks
1 small bunch spring onions,
   trimmed and shredded
18 ready-made Chinese
   pancakes, warmed

Preheat the oven to 220°C/425°F/Gas Mark 7, 15 minutes before cooking. Discard the stones from the plums and place in a saucepan with the butter, star anise, ginger, brown sugar and orange zest and juice. Season to taste with pepper. Cook over a gentle heat until the sugar has dissolved. Bring to the boil, then reduce heat and simmer for 15 minutes, stirring occasionally until the plums are soft and the mixture is thick. Remove the star anise. Leave to cool.

Using a fork, prick the duck legs all over. Place in a large bowl and pour boiling water over to remove some of the fat. Drain, pat dry on absorbent kitchen paper and leave until cold.

Mix together the soy sauce, dark brown sugar and the ½ teaspoon of salt. Rub this mixture generously over the duck legs. Transfer to a wire rack set over a roasting tin and roast in the preheated oven for 30–40 minutes, or until well cooked and the skin is browned and crisp. Remove from the oven and leave to rest for 10 minutes.

Shred the duck meat using a fork to hold the hot duck leg and another to remove the meat. Transfer to a warmed serving platter with the cucumber and spring onions. Serve immediately with the plum compote and warmed pancakes.

Try this: FOR AN ALTERNATIVE: 268   FOR ENTERTAINING: 318

Seared Duck
with Pickled Plums

SERVES 4

4 small skinless, boneless
    duck breasts
2 garlic cloves, peeled
    and crushed
1 tsp hot chilli sauce
2 tsp clear honey
2 tsp dark brown sugar
juice of 1 lime

1 tbsp dark soy sauce
6 large plums, halved and
    stones removed
50 g/2 oz caster sugar
50 ml/2 fl oz white
    wine vinegar
¼ tsp dried chilli flakes
¼ tsp ground cinnamon

1 tbsp sunflower oil
150 ml/¼ pint chicken stock
2 tbsp oyster sauce
sprigs of fresh flat leaf
    parsley, to garnish
freshly cooked noodles,
    to serve

Cut a few deep slashes in each duck breast and place in a shallow dish. Mix together the garlic, chilli sauce, honey, brown sugar, lime juice and soy sauce. Spread over the duck and leave to marinate in the refrigerator for 4 hours or overnight, if time permits, turning occasionally.

Place the plums in a saucepan with the caster sugar, white wine vinegar, chilli flakes and cinnamon and bring to the boil. Simmer gently for 5 minutes, or until the plums have just softened, then leave to cool.

Remove the duck from the marinade and pat dry with absorbent kitchen paper. Reserve the marinade. Heat a wok or large frying pan, add the oil and when hot, brown the duck on both sides. Pour in the stock, oyster sauce and reserved marinade and simmer for 5 minutes. Remove the duck and keep warm.

Remove the plums from their liquid and reserve. Pour the liquid into the duck sauce, bring to the boil, then simmer, uncovered, for 5 minutes, or until reduced and thickened. Arrange the duck on warmed plates. Divide the plums between the plates and spoon over the sauce. Garnish with parsley and serve immediately with noodles.

Try this: FOR AN ALTERNATIVE: 334 FOR ENTERTAINING: 228

Duck & Exotic Fruit Stir Fry

SERVES 4

4 duck breast fillets,
   skinned removed and
   cut into strips
½ tsp Chinese five
   spice powder
2 tbsp soy sauce
1 tbsp sesame oil
1 tbsp groundnut oil

2 celery stalks, trimmed
   and diced
225 g can pineapples
   chunks, drained
1 mango, peeled, stoned
   and cut into chunks
125 g/4 oz lychees, peeled if
   fresh, stoned and halved

125 ml/4 fl oz chicken stock
2 tbsp tomato paste
2 tbsp plum sauce
2 tsp wine vinegar
pinch of soft brown sugar
toasted nuts, to garnish
steamed rice, to serve

Place the duck strips in a shallow bowl. Mix together the Chinese five spice powder, soy sauce and sesame oil, pour over the duck and marinate for 2 hours in the refrigerator. Stir occasionally during marinating. Remove the duck from the marinade and reserve.

Heat the wok, add the oil and when hot, stir-fry the marinated duck strips for 4 minutes. Remove from the wok and reserve.

Add the celery to the wok and stir-fry for 2 minutes, then add the pineapple, mango and lychees and stir-fry for a further 3 minutes. Return the duck to the wok.

Mix together the chicken stock, tomato paste, plum sauce, wine vinegar and a pinch of brown sugar. Add to the wok, bring to the boil and simmer, stirring, for 2 minutes. Sprinkle with the nuts and serve immediately with the freshly steamed rice.

Try this: FOR AN ALTERNATIVE: 320   FOR ENTERTAINING: 322

Hoisin Duck & Greens Stir Fry

SERVES 4

350 g/12 oz duck breasts, skinned and cut into strips
1 medium egg white, beaten
½ tsp salt
1 tsp sesame oil
2 tsp cornflour
2 tbsp groundnut oil

2 tbsp freshly grated root ginger
50 g/2 oz bamboo shoots
50 g/2 oz fine green beans, trimmed
50 g/2 oz pak choi, trimmed
2 tbsp hoisin sauce

1 tsp Chinese rice wine or dry sherry
zest and juice of ½ orange
strips of orange zest, to garnish
freshly steamed egg noodles, to serve

Place the duck strips in a shallow dish, then add the egg white, salt, sesame oil and cornflour. Stir lightly until the duck is coated in the mixture. Cover and chill in the refrigerator for 20 minutes.

Heat the wok until very hot and add the oil. Remove the wok from the heat and add the duck, stirring continuously to prevent the duck from sticking to the wok. Add the ginger and stir-fry for 2 minutes. Add the bamboo shoots, the green beans and the pak choi, and stir-fry for 1–2 minutes until wilted.

Mix together the hoisin sauce, the Chinese rice wine or sherry and the orange zest and juice. Pour into the wok and stir to coat the duck and vegetables. Stir-fry for 1–2 minutes, or until the duck and vegetables are tender. Garnish with the strips of orange zest and serve immediately with freshly steamed egg noodles.

Try this: FOR AN ALTERNATIVE: 350   FOR ENTERTAINING: 368

Teriyaki Duck with Plum Chutney

SERVES 4

4 tbsp Japanese soy sauce
4 tbsp dry sherry
2 garlic cloves, peeled and finely chopped
2.5 cm/1 inch piece fresh root ginger, peeled and finely chopped
350 g/12 oz skinless duck breast fillets, cut in chunks

2 tbsp groundnut oil
225 g/8 oz carrots, peeled and cut into fine strips
½ cucumber, cut into strips
5 spring onions, trimmed and shredded
toasted almonds, to garnish
freshly cooked egg noodles, to serve

For the plum chutney:
25 g/1 oz butter
1 red onion, peeled and finely chopped
2 tsp soft brown sugar
4 plums, stoned and halved
zest and juice of ½ orange
50 g/2 oz raisins

Mix together the soy sauce, sherry, garlic and ginger and pour into a shallow dish. Add the duck strips and stir until coated in the marinade. Cover and leave in the refrigerator for 30 minutes.

Meanwhile, make the plum chutney. Melt the butter in a wok, add the onion and sugar and cook gently over a low heat for 20 minutes. Add the plums, orange zest and juice and simmer for 10 minutes, then stir in the raisins. Spoon into a small bowl and wipe the wok clean. Drain the duck, reserving the marinade.

Heat the wok, add the oil and when hot, add the carrots, cucumber and spring onions. Stir-fry for 2 minutes, or until tender. Remove and reserve.

Add the drained duck to the wok and stir-fry over a high heat for 2 minutes. Return the vegetables to the wok and add the reserved marinade. Stir-fry briefly, until heated through. Garnish the duck with the toasted almonds and serve immediately with freshly cooked noodles and the plum chutney.

Try this: FOR AN ALTERNATIVE: 302   FOR ENTERTAINING: 158

Duck in Crispy Wonton Shells

SERVES 4

2 x 175 g/6 oz duck breasts
2 tbsp Chinese five
   spice powder
2 tbsp Szechuan peppercorns
1 tsp whole black
   peppercorns

3 tbsp cumin seeds
5 tbsp sea salt
6 slices fresh root ginger
6 spring onions,
   roughly chopped
1 tbsp cornflour

1 litre/1¾ pints vegetable oil
   for frying
16 wonton wrappers
5 cm/2 inch piece cucumber,
   cut into fine strips
125 ml/4 fl oz hoisin sauce

Rinse the duck and dry thoroughly with absorbent kitchen paper. Place the Chinese five spice powder, peppercorns, cumin seeds and salt in a pestle and mortar and crush. Rub the spice mix all over the duck. Wrap in clingfilm and refrigerate for 24 hours.

Place a rack in the wok and pour in boiling water to a depth of 5 cm/2 inches. Place the duck breasts with the ginger slices and 3 chopped spring onions in a heatproof dish on top of the rack. Cover and steam for 40–50 minutes, or until the duck is cooked. Pour off any excess fat from time to time and add more water if necessary. Remove the duck and leave until cooled.

Dust the duck breasts with cornflour, shaking off the excess. Heat the wok, add the oil and, when almost smoking, deep-fry the duck for 8 minutes. Drain, then shred the meat into bite-sized pieces. Shred the remaining spring onions.

Reheat the oil until smoking. Working with one wonton at a time, insert two wooden skewers into each one, hold in a taco shape and lower into the oil. Hold in the oil until crisp and golden brown. Drain on absorbent kitchen paper. Repeat with the remaining wontons. Fill the wontons with the duck, topped with the spring onions, cucumber and hoisin sauce and serve immediately.

Try this: FOR AN ALTERNATIVE: 242 FOR ENTERTAINING: 378

Stir–fried Duck with Cashews

SERVES 4

450 g/1 lb duck breast,
  skinned
3 tbsp groundnut oil
1 garlic clove, peeled and
  finely chopped
1 tsp freshly grated
  ginger root

1 carrot, peeled and sliced
125 g/4 oz mangetout,
  trimmed
2 tsp Chinese rice wine
  or dry sherry
1 tbsp light soy sauce
1 tsp cornflour

50 g/2 oz unsalted cashew
  nuts, roasted
1 spring onion, trimmed
  and finely chopped
1 spring onion, shredded
boiled or steamed rice,
  to serve

Trim the duck breasts, discarding any fat and slice thickly. Heat the wok, add 2 tablespoons of the oil and when hot, add the sliced duck breast. Cook for 3–4 minutes or until sealed. Using a slotted spoon, remove from the wok and leave to drain on absorbent kitchen paper.

Wipe the wok clean and return to the heat. Add the remaining oil and when hot, add the garlic and ginger. Stir-fry for 30 seconds, then add the carrot and mangetout. Stir-fry for a further 2 minutes, then pour in the Chinese rice wine or sherry and soy sauce.

Blend the cornflour with 1 teaspoon of water and stir into the wok. Mix well and bring to the boil. Return the duck slices to the wok and simmer for 5 minutes, or until the meat and vegetables are tender. Add the cashews, then remove the wok from the heat.

Sprinkle over the chopped and shredded spring onion and serve immediately with plain boiled or steamed rice.

Try this: FOR AN ALTERNATIVE: 352   FOR ENTERTAINING: 298

Asian Food: Vegetables & Salads

Curried Parsnip Soup

SERVES 4

1 tsp cumin seeds
2 tsp coriander seeds
1 tsp oil
1 onion, peeled
    and chopped
1 garlic clove,
    peeled and crushed

½ tsp turmeric
¼ tsp chilli powder
1 cinnamon stick
450 g/1 lb parsnips, peeled
    and chopped
1 litre/1¾ pint
    vegetable stock

salt and freshly ground
    black pepper
2–3 tbsp natural yogurt,
    to serve
fresh coriander leaves,
    to garnish

In a small frying pan, dry-fry the cumin and coriander seeds over a moderately high heat for 1–2 minutes. Shake the pan during cooking until the seeds are lightly toasted. Reserve until cooled. Grind the toasted seeds in a pestle and mortar.

Heat the oil in a saucepan. Cook the onion until softened and starting to turn golden. Add the garlic, turmeric, chilli powder and cinnamon stick to the pan. Continue to cook for a further minute. Add the parsnips and stir well. Pour in the stock and bring to the boil. Cover and simmer for 15 minutes or until the parsnips are cooked.

Allow the soup to cool. Once cooled, remove the cinnamon stick and discard. Blend the soup in a food processor until very smooth.

Transfer to a saucepan and reheat gently. Season to taste with salt and pepper. Garnish with fresh coriander and serve immediately with the yogurt.

Sweetcorn Cakes

SERVES 6–8

250 g/9 oz self-raising flour
3 tbsp Thai red curry paste
2 tbsp light soy sauce
2 tsp sugar
2 kaffir lime leaves,
    finely shredded
12 fine French beans,
    trimmed, finely
    chopped and blanched

340 g can sweetcorn, drained
salt and freshly ground
    black pepper
2 medium eggs
50 g/2 oz fresh white
    breadcrumbs
vegetable oil for deep-frying

For the dipping sauce:
2 tbsp hoisin sauce
1 tbsp soft light brown sugar
1 tbsp sesame oil

To serve:
halved cucumber slices
spring onions, sliced
    diagonally

Place the flour in a bowl, make a well in the centre, then add the curry paste, soy sauce and the sugar together with the shredded kaffir lime leaves, French beans and sweetcorn. Season to taste with salt and pepper, then beat 1 of the eggs and add to the mixture. Stir in with a fork adding 1–2 tablespoons of cold water to form a stiff dough. Knead lightly on a floured surface and form into a ball.

Divide the mixture into 16 pieces and shape into small balls, then flatten to form cakes about 1 cm/½ inch thick and 7.5 cm/3 inches in diameter. Beat the remaining egg and pour into a shallow dish. Dip the cakes first in a little beaten egg, then in the breadcrumbs until lightly coated.

Heat the oil in either a wok or deep-fat fryer to 180°C/350°F and deep-fry the cakes for 2–3 minutes or until golden brown in colour. Using a slotted spoon, remove and drain on absorbent kitchen paper.

Meanwhile, blend the hoisin sauce, sugar, 1 tablespoon of water and the sesame oil together until smooth and pour into a small bowl. Serve immediately with the sweetcorn cakes, cucumber and spring onions.

Try this: FOR AN ALTERNATIVE: 240   FOR ENTERTAINING: 78

Hot & Sour Mushroom Soup

SERVES 4

4 tbsp sunflower oil
3 garlic cloves, peeled and
    finely chopped
3 shallots, peeled and
    finely chopped
2 large red chillies,
    deseeded and
    finely chopped
1 tbsp soft brown sugar
large pinch of salt

1 litre/1¾ pints
    vegetable stock
250 g/9 oz Thai fragrant rice
5 kaffir lime leaves, torn
2 tbsp soy sauce
grated rind and juice
    of 1 lemon
250 g/9 oz oyster
    mushrooms, wiped and
    cut into pieces

2 tbsp freshly
    chopped coriander

To garnish:
2 green chillies, deseeded
    and finely chopped
3 spring onions, trimmed
    and finely chopped

Heat the oil in a frying pan, add the garlic and shallots and cook until golden brown and starting to crisp. Remove from the pan and reserve. Add the chillies to the pan and cook until they start to change colour.

Place the garlic, shallots and chillies in a food processor or blender and blend to a smooth purée with 150 ml/¼ pint water. Pour the purée back into the pan, add the sugar with a large pinch of salt, then cook gently, stirring, until dark in colour. Take care not to burn the mixture.

Pour the stock into a large saucepan, add the garlic purée, rice, lime leaves, soy sauce and the lemon rind and juice. Bring to the boil, then reduce the heat, cover and simmer gently for about 10 minutes.

Add the mushrooms and simmer for a further 10 minutes, or until the mushrooms and rice are tender. Remove the lime leaves, stir in the chopped coriander and ladle into bowls. Place the chopped green chillies and spring onions in small bowls and serve separately to sprinkle on top of the soup.

Try this: FOR AN ALTERNATIVE: 246   FOR ENTERTAINING: 82

Spicy Filled Naan Bread

MAKES 6

400 g/14 oz strong
  white flour
1 tsp salt
1 tsp easy-blend dried yeast
15 g/½ oz ghee or unsalted
  butter, melted
1 tsp clear honey
200 ml/7 fl oz warm water

For the filling:
25 g/1 oz ghee or unsalted
  butter
1 small onion, peeled and
  finely chopped
1 garlic clove, peeled
  and crushed
1 tsp ground coriander

1 tsp ground cumin
2 tsp grated fresh
  root ginger
pinch of chilli powder
pinch of ground cinnamon
salt and freshly ground
  black pepper

Preheat the oven to 220°C/450°F/Gas Mark 8, 15 minutes before baking and place a large baking sheet in to heat up. Sift the flour and salt into a large bowl. Stir in the yeast and make a well in the centre. Add the ghee or melted butter, honey and the warm water. Mix to a soft dough. Knead the dough on a lightly floured surface until smooth and elastic. Put in a lightly oiled bowl, cover with clingfilm and leave to rise for 1 hour, or until doubled in size.

For the filling, melt the ghee or butter in a frying pan and gently cook the onion for about 5 minutes. Stir in the garlic and spices and season to taste with salt and pepper. Cook for a further 6–7 minutes, until soft. Remove from the heat, stir in 1 tablespoon of water and leave to cool.

Briefly knead the dough, then divide into six pieces. Roll out each piece of dough to 12.5 cm/ 5 inch rounds. Spoon the filling on to one half of each round. Fold over and press the edges together to seal. Re-roll to shape into flat ovals, about 16 cm/6½ inches long.

Cover with oiled clingfilm and leave to rise for about 15 minutes. Transfer the breads to the hot baking sheet and cook in the preheated oven for 10–12 minutes, until puffed up and lightly browned. Serve hot.

Try this: FOR AN ALTERNATIVE: 190 FOR ENTERTAINING: 178

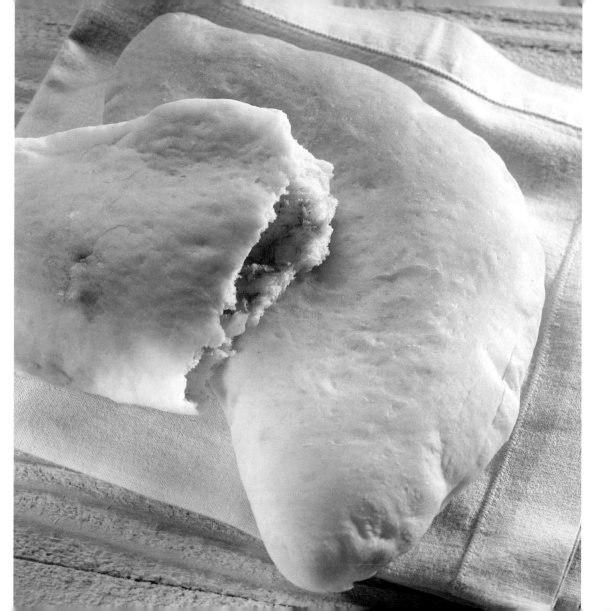

Chinese Leaves with Sweet & Sour Sauce

SERVES 4

1 head Chinese leaves	2 tbsp brown sugar	3 tbsp sunflower oil
200 g pack pak choi	3 tbsp red wine vinegar	15 g/½ oz butter
1 tbsp cornflour	3 tbsp orange juice	1 tsp salt
1 tbsp soy sauce	2 tbsp tomato purée	2 tbsp toasted sesame seeds

Discard any tough outer leaves and stalks from the Chinese leaves and pak choi and wash well. Drain thoroughly and pat dry with absorbent kitchen paper. Shred the Chinese leaves and pak choi lengthways. Reserve.

In a small bowl, blend the cornflour with 4 tablespoons of water. Add the soy sauce, sugar, vinegar, orange juice and tomato purée and stir until blended thoroughly.

Pour the sauce into a small saucepan and bring to the boil. Simmer gently for 2–3 minutes, or until the sauce is thickened and smooth.

Meanwhile, heat a wok or large frying pan and add the sunflower oil and butter. When melted, add the prepared Chinese leaves and pak choi, sprinkle with the salt and stir-fry for 2 minutes. Reduce the heat and cook gently for a further 1–2 minutes or until tender.

Transfer the Chinese leaves and pak choi to a warmed serving platter and drizzle over the warm sauce. Sprinkle with the toasted sesame seeds and serve immediately.

Try this: FOR AN ALTERNATIVE: 214 FOR ENTERTAINING: 368

Bean & Cashew Stir Fry

SERVES 4

3 tbsp sunflower oil
1 onion, peeled and
  finely chopped
1 celery stalk, trimmed
  and chopped
2.5 cm/1 inch piece fresh
  root ginger, peeled
  and grated
2 garlic cloves, peeled
  and crushed

1 red chilli, deseeded and
  finely chopped
175 g/6 oz fine French beans,
  trimmed and halved
175 g/6 oz mangetout, sliced
  diagonally into 3
75 g/3 oz unsalted
  cashew nuts
1 tsp brown sugar
125 ml/4 fl oz

vegetable stock
2 tbsp dry sherry
1 tbsp light soy sauce
1 tsp red wine vinegar
salt and freshly ground
  black pepper
freshly chopped coriander,
  to garnish

Heat a wok or large frying pan, add the oil and when hot, add the onion and celery and stir-fry gently for 3–4 minutes or until softened.

Add the ginger, garlic and chilli to the wok and stir-fry for 30 seconds. Stir in the French beans and mangetout together with the cashew nuts and continue to stir-fry for 1–2 minutes, or until the nuts are golden brown.

Dissolve the sugar in the stock, then blend with the sherry, soy sauce and vinegar. Stir into the bean mixture and bring to the boil. Simmer gently, stirring occasionally for 3–4 minutes, or until the beans and mangetout are tender but still crisp and the sauce has thickened slightly.

Season to taste with salt and pepper. Transfer to a warmed serving bowl or spoon on to individual plates. Sprinkle with freshly chopped coriander and serve immediately.

Try this: FOR AN ALTERNATIVE: 298   FOR ENTERTAINING: 338

Fried Rice with Bamboo Shoots & Ginger

SERVES 4

4 tbsp sunflower oil
1 onion, peeled and
    finely chopped
225 g/8 oz long-grain rice
3 garlic cloves, peeled
    and cut into slivers
2.5 cm/1 inch piece fresh
    root ginger, peeled
    and grated

3 spring onions, trimmed
    and chopped
450 ml/¾ pint
    vegetable stock
125 g/4 oz button
    mushrooms, wiped
    and halved
75 g/3 oz frozen peas,
    thawed

2 tbsp light soy sauce
500 g can bamboo shoots,
    drained and thinly sliced
salt and freshly ground
    black pepper
cayenne pepper, to taste
fresh coriander leaves,
    to garnish

Heat a wok, add the oil and when hot, add the onion and cook gently for 3–4 minutes, then add the long-grain rice and cook for 3–4 minutes or until golden, stirring frequently.

Add the garlic, ginger and chopped spring onions to the wok and stir well. Pour the chicken stock into a small saucepan and bring to the boil. Carefully ladle the hot stock into the wok, stir well, then simmer gently for 10 minutes or until most of the liquid has been absorbed.

Stir the button mushrooms, peas and soy sauce into the wok and continue to cook for a further 5 minutes, or until the rice is tender, adding a little extra stock if necessary.

Add the bamboo shoots to the wok and carefully stir in. Season to taste with salt, pepper and cayenne pepper. Cook for 2–3 minutes or until heated through. Tip on to a warmed serving dish, garnish with coriander leaves and serve immediately.

Try this: FOR AN ALTERNATIVE: 358   FOR ENTERTAINING: 322

Vegetables in Coconut Milk with Rice Noodles

SERVES 4

75 g/3 oz creamed coconut
1 tsp salt
2 tbsp sunflower oil
2 garlic cloves, peeled and finely chopped
2 red peppers, deseeded and cut into thin strips
2.5 cm/1 inch piece of fresh root ginger, peeled and cut into thin strips
125 g/4 oz baby sweetcorn
2 tsp cornflour
2 medium ripe but still firm avocados
1 small Cos lettuce, cut into thick strips
freshly cooked rice noodles, to serve

Roughly chop the creamed coconut, place in a bowl with the salt, then pour over 600 ml/1 pint of boiling water. Stir until the coconut has dissolved completely and reserve.

Heat a wok or large frying pan, add the oil and when hot, add the chopped garlic, sliced peppers and ginger. Cook for 30 seconds, then cover and cook very gently for 10 minutes or until the peppers are soft.

Pour in the reserved coconut milk and bring to the boil. Stir in the baby sweetcorn, cover and simmer for 5 minutes. Blend the cornflour with 2 teaspoons of water, pour into the wok and cook, stirring, for 2 minutes or until thickened slightly.

Cut the avocados in half, peel, remove the stone and slice. Add to the wok with the lettuce strips and stir until well mixed and heated through. Serve immediately on a bed of rice noodles.

Try this: FOR AN ALTERNATIVE: 26   FOR ENTERTAINING: 164

Basmati Rice with Saffron & Broad Beans

SERVES 4

1 medium egg
2 tbsp olive oil
1 tbsp freshly chopped
    mixed herbs
salt and freshly ground

black pepper
200 g/7 oz basmati rice
50 g/2 oz butter
1 small onion, peeled and
    finely chopped

1 garlic clove, peeled and
    finely chopped
large pinch saffron strands
225 g/8 oz shelled broad
    beans, blanched

Beat the egg with 1 teaspoon of olive oil and the herbs. Season lightly with salt and pepper. Heat the remaining teaspoon of olive oil in a wok or small frying wok. Pour half the egg mixture into the pan, tilting it to coat the bottom. Cook gently until set on top. Flip over and cook for a further 30 seconds. Transfer to a plate and repeat, using the remaining mixture, then reserve.

Wash the rice in several changes of water until the water remains relatively clear. Add the drained rice to a large saucepan of boiling salted water and cook for 12–15 minutes until tender. Drain well and reserve.

Heat the butter with the remaining oil in a wok and add the onion and garlic. Cook gently for 3–4 minutes until the onion is softened. Add the saffron and stir well. Add the drained rice and stir before adding the broad beans. Cook for a further 2–3 minutes, or until heated through.

Meanwhile, roll the egg pancakes into cigar shapes then slice crossways into strips. To serve, divide the rice between individual serving bowls and top with the egg strips.

Try this: FOR AN ALTERNATIVE: 370   FOR ENTERTAINING: 374

Cold Sesame Noodles

SERVES 4–8

450 g/1 lb buckwheat
(soba) noodles or
wholewheat spaghetti
salt
1 tbsp sesame oil
1 tbsp groundnut oil
1 green pepper, deseeded
and thinly sliced
125 g/4 oz daikon (mooli),
cut into julienne strips

125 g/4 oz mangetout or
green beans, trimmed
and sliced
2 garlic cloves, peeled
and finely chopped
2 tbsp soy sauce, or to taste
1 tbsp cider vinegar
2 tbsp sweet chilli sauce,
or to taste
2 tsp sugar

75 g/3 oz peanut butter
6–8 spring onions, trimmed
and diagonally sliced

To garnish:
toasted sesame seeds
julienne strips of cucumber

Bring a large pan of lightly salted water to a rolling boil. Add the noodles or spaghetti and cook according to the packet instructions, or until 'al dente'. Drain, rinse and drain again, then toss in the sesame oil and reserve.

Heat the groundnut oil in a wok or large frying pan over a high heat. Add the green pepper, daikon and mangetout or green beans and stir-fry for 1 minute. Stir in the garlic and cook for 30 seconds.

Add the soy sauce to the pan with the vinegar, chilli sauce, sugar, peanut butter and 50 ml/ 2 fl oz of hot water. Simmer, stirring constantly, until the peanut butter is smooth, adding a little more water if necessary and adjusting the seasoning to taste.

Add the spring onions and the reserved noodles or spaghetti to the peanut sauce and cook, stirring, for 2–3 minutes, or until heated through. Tip the mixture into a large serving bowl and allow to cool to room temperature, stirring occasionally. Garnish with the toasted sesame seeds and cucumber julienne strips before serving.

Try this: FOR AN ALTERNATIVE: 362   FOR ENTERTAINING: 310

Singapore Noodles

SERVES 4

225 g/8 oz thin round
    egg noodles
3 tbsp groundnut or
    vegetable oil
125 g/4 oz field mushrooms,
    wiped and thinly sliced
2.5 cm/1 inch piece root
    ginger, peeled and
    finely chopped
1 red chilli, deseeded and
    thinly sliced

1 red pepper, deseeded
    and thinly sliced
2 garlic cloves, peeled
    and crushed
1 medium courgette,
    cut in half lengthwise
    and diagonally sliced
4-6 spring onions, trimmed
    and thinly sliced
50 g/2 oz frozen garden
    peas, thawed

1 tbsp curry paste
2 tbsp tomato ketchup
salt or soy sauce
125 g/4 oz beansprouts,
    rinsed and drained

To garnish:
sesame seeds
fresh coriander leaves

Bring a large pan of lightly salted water to a rolling boil. Add the noodles and cook according to the packet instructions, or until 'al dente'. Drain thoroughly and toss with 1 tablespoon of the oil. Heat the remaining oil in a wok or large frying pan over high heat. Add the mushrooms, ginger, chilli and red pepper and stir-fry for 2 minutes. Add the garlic, courgettes, spring onions and garden peas and stir lightly.

Push the vegetables to one side and add the curry paste, tomato ketchup and about 125 ml/4 fl oz hot water. Season to taste with salt or a few drops of soy sauce and allow to boil vigorously, stirring, until the paste is smooth.

Stir the reserved egg noodles and the beansprouts into the vegetable mixture and stir-fry until coated with the paste and thoroughly heated through. Season with more soy sauce if necessary, then turn into a large warmed serving bowl or spoon on to individual plates. Garnish with sesame seeds and coriander leaves. Serve immediately.

Try this: FOR AN ALTERNATIVE: 356   FOR ENTERTAINING: 314

Thai Noodles & Vegetables with Tofu

SERVES 4

225 g/8 oz firm tofu
2 tbsp soy sauce
rind of 1 lime, grated
2 lemon grass stalks
1 red chilli
1 litre/1¾ pint
   vegetable stock
2 slices fresh root
   ginger, peeled

2 garlic cloves, peeled
2 sprigs of fresh coriander
175 g/6 oz dried thread
   egg noodles
125 g/4 oz shiitake or
   button mushrooms,
   sliced if large
2 carrots, peeled and
   cut into matchsticks

125 g/4 oz mangetout
125 g/4 oz bok choy or
   other Chinese leaf
1 tbsp freshly
   chopped coriander
salt and freshly ground
   black pepper
coriander sprigs,
   to garnish

Drain the tofu well and cut into cubes. Put into a shallow dish with the soy sauce and lime rind. Stir well to coat and leave to marinate for 30 minutes.

Meanwhile, put the lemon grass and chilli on a chopping board and bruise with the side of a large knife, ensuring the blade is pointing away from you. Put the vegetable stock in a large saucepan and add the lemon grass, chilli, ginger, garlic, and coriander. Bring to the boil, cover and simmer gently for 20 minutes.

Strain the stock into a clean pan. Return to the boil and add the noodles, tofu and its marinade and the mushrooms. Simmer gently for 4 minutes.

Add the carrots, mangetout, bok choy, coriander and simmer for a further 3–4 minutes until the vegetables are just tender. Season to taste with salt and pepper. Garnish with coriander sprigs. Serve immediately.

Try this: FOR AN ALTERNATIVE: 60   FOR ENTERTAINING: 98

Pad Thai Noodles with Mushrooms

SERVES 4

125 g/4 oz flat rice noodles
   or rice vermicelli
1 tbsp vegetable oil
2 garlic cloves, peeled
   and finely chopped
1 medium egg,
   lightly beaten
225 g/8 oz mixed

mushrooms, including
   shiitake, oyster, field,
   brown and wild
   mushrooms
2 tbsp lemon juice
1½ tbsp Thai fish sauce
½ tsp sugar
½ tsp cayenne pepper

2 spring onions, trimmed
   and cut into 2.5 cm/1
   inch pieces
50 g/2 oz fresh beansprouts

To garnish:
chopped roasted peanuts
freshly chopped coriander

Cook the noodles according to the packet instructions. Drain well and reserve.

Heat a wok or large frying pan. Add the oil and garlic. Fry until just golden. Add the egg and stir quickly to break it up.

Cook for a few seconds before adding the noodles and mushrooms. Scrape down the sides of the pan to ensure they mix with the egg and garlic.

Add the lemon juice, fish sauce, sugar, cayenne pepper, spring onions and half of the beansprouts, stirring quickly all the time. Cook over a high heat for a further 2–3 minutes until everything is heated through.

Turn on to a serving plate. Top with the remaining beansprouts. Garnish with the chopped peanuts and coriander and serve immediately.

Try this: FOR AN ALTERNATIVE: 270   FOR ENTERTAINING: 182

Chinese Salad with Soy & Ginger Dressing

SERVES 4

1 head of Chinese cabbage	125 g/4 oz beansprouts	2.5 cm/1 inch piece root
200 g can water	2 tbsp freshly	ginger, peeled and
chestnuts, drained	chopped coriander	finely grated
6 spring onions, trimmed	For the soy and ginger	zest and juice of 1 lemon
4 ripe but firm	dressing:	salt and freshly ground
cherry tomatoes	2 tbsp sunflower oil	black pepper
125 g/4 oz mangetout	4 tbsp light soy sauce	crusty white bread, to serve

Rinse and finely shred the Chinese cabbage and place in a serving dish. Slice the water chestnuts into small slivers and cut the spring onions diagonally into 2.5 cm/1 inch lengths, then split lengthwise into thin strips.

Cut the tomatoes in half and then slice each half into three wedges and reserve.

Simmer the mangetout in boiling water for 2 minutes until beginning to soften, drain and cut in half diagonally.

Arrange the water chestnuts, spring onions, mangetout, tomatoes and beansprouts on top of the shredded Chinese cabbage. Garnish with the freshly chopped coriander.

Make the dressing by whisking all the ingredients together in a small bowl until mixed thoroughly. Serve with the bread and the salad.

Mixed Grain Pilaf

SERVES 4

2 tbsp olive oil
1 garlic clove, peeled
  and crushed
½ tsp ground turmeric
125 g/4 oz mixed long-grain
  and wild rice
50 g/2 oz red lentils
300 ml/½ pint

vegetable stock
200 g can chopped tomatoes
5 cm/2 inch piece
  cinnamon stick
salt and freshly ground
  black pepper
400 g can mixed beans,
  drained and rinsed

15 g/½ oz butter
1 bunch spring onions,
  trimmed and finely sliced
3 medium eggs
4 tbsp freshly chopped herbs,
  such as parsley and chervil
sprigs of fresh dill,
  to garnish

Heat 1 tablespoon of the oil in a saucepan. Add the garlic and turmeric and cook for a few seconds. Stir in the rice and lentils. Add the stock, tomatoes and cinnamon. Season to taste with salt and pepper. Stir once and bring to the boil. Lower the heat, cover and simmer for 20 minutes, until most of the stock is absorbed and the rice and lentils are tender.

Stir in the beans, replace the lid and leave to stand for 2–3 minutes to allow the beans to heat through. While the rice is cooking, heat the remaining oil and butter in a frying pan. Add the spring onions and cook for 4–5 minutes, until soft. Lightly beat the eggs with 2 tablespoons of the herbs, then season with salt and pepper.

Pour the egg mixture over the spring onions. Stir gently with a spatula over a low heat, drawing the mixture from the sides to the centre as the omelette sets. When almost set, stop stirring and cook for about 30 seconds until golden underneath.

Remove the omelette from the pan, roll up and slice into thin strips. Fluff the rice up with a fork and remove the cinnamon stick. Spoon onto serving plates, top with strips of omelette and the remaining chopped herbs. Garnish with sprigs of dill and serve.

Try this: FOR AN ALTERNATIVE: 160   FOR ENTERTAINING: 130

Vegetable Tempura

SERVES 4-6

125 g/4 oz rice flour
75 g/3 oz plain flour
4 tsp baking powder
1 tbsp dried
   mustard powder
2 tsp semolina
salt and freshly ground

black pepper
300 ml/½ pint groundnut oil
125 g/4 oz courgette,
   trimmed and thickly sliced
125 g/4 oz mangetout
125 g/4 oz baby sweetcorn
4 small red onions, peeled

and quartered
1 large red pepper,
   deseeded and cut into
   2.5 cm/1 inch wide strips
light soy sauce,
   to serve

Sift the rice flour and the plain flour into a large bowl, then sift in the baking powder and dried mustard powder.

Stir the semolina into the flour mixture and season to taste with salt and pepper. Gradually beat in 300 ml/½ pint cold water to produce a thin coating batter. Leave to stand at room temperature for 30 minutes.

Heat a wok or large frying pan, add the oil and heat to 180°C/350°F. Working in batches and using a slotted spoon, dip the vegetables in the batter until well coated, then drop them carefully into the hot oil. Cook each batch for 2–3 minutes or until golden. Drain on absorbent kitchen paper and keep warm while cooking the remaining batches.

Transfer the vegetables to a warmed serving platter and serve immediately with the light soy sauce to use as a dipping sauce.

Try this: FOR AN ALTERNATIVE: 378   FOR ENTERTAINING: 146

Oriental Noodle & Peanut Salad with Coriander

SERVES 4

350 g/12 oz rice vermicelli
1 litre/1¾ pints light
chicken stock
2 tsp sesame oil
2 tbsp light soy sauce
8 spring onions

3 tbsp groundnut oil
2 hot green chillis, deseeded
and thinly sliced
25 g/1 oz roughly chopped
coriander
2 tbsp freshly chopped mint

125 g/4 oz cucumber,
finely chopped
40 g/1½ oz beansprouts
40 g/1½ oz roasted peanuts,
roughly chopped

Put the noodles into a large bowl. Bring the stock to the boil and immediately pour over the noodles. Leave to soak for 4 minutes, or according to the packet directions. Drain well, discarding the stock or saving it for another use. Mix together the sesame oil and soy sauce and pour over the hot noodles. Toss well to coat and leave until cold.

Trim and thinly slice 4 of the spring onions. Heat the oil in a wok over a low heat. Add the spring onions and, as soon as they sizzle, remove from the heat and leave to cool. When cold, toss with the noodles.

On a chopping board, cut the remaining spring onions lengthways 4–6 times, leave in a bowl of cold water until tassels form. Serve the noodles in individual bowls, each dressed with a little chilli, coriander, mint, cucumber, beansprouts and peanuts. Garnish with the spring onion tassels and serve.

Try this: FOR AN ALTERNATIVE: 368   FOR ENTERTAINING: 360

Vegetable Thai Spring Rolls

SERVES 4

50 g/2 oz cellophane
 vermicelli
4 dried shiitake mushrooms
1 tbsp groundnut oil
2 medium carrots, peeled
 and cut into fine
 matchsticks
125 g/4 oz mangetout, cut
 lengthways into fine strips

3 spring onions, trimmed
 and chopped
125 g/4 oz canned bamboo
 shoots, cut into fine
 matchsticks
1 cm/½ inch piece fresh root
 ginger, peeled
 and grated
1 tbsp light soy sauce

1 medium egg, separated
salt and freshly ground
 black pepper
20 spring roll wrappers,
 each about 12.5 cm/
 5 inch square
vegetable oil for deep-frying
spring onion tassels,
 to garnish

Place the vermicelli in a bowl and pour over enough boiling water to cover. Leave to soak for 5 minutes or until softened, then drain. Cut into 7.5 cm/3 inch lengths. Soak the shiitake mushrooms in almost boiling water for 15 minutes, drain, discard the stalks and slice thinly. Heat a wok or large frying pan, add the groundnut oil and when hot, add the carrots and stir-fry for 1 minute. Add the mangetout and spring onions and stir-fry for 2–3 minutes or until tender. Tip the vegetables into a bowl and leave to cool. Stir the vermicelli and shiitake mushrooms into the cooled vegetables with the bamboo shoots, ginger, soy sauce and egg yolk. Season to taste with salt and pepper and mix thoroughly.

Brush the edges of a spring roll wrapper with a little beaten egg white. Spoon 2 teaspoons of the vegetable filling on to the wrapper, in a 7.5 cm/3 inch log shape 2.5 cm/1 inch from one edge. Fold the wrapper edge over the filling, then fold in the right and left sides. Brush the folded edges with more egg white and roll up neatly. Place on an oiled baking sheet, seam-side down and make the rest of the spring rolls. Heat the oil in a heavy-based saucepan or deep-fat fryer to 180°C/350°F. Deep-fry the spring rolls, six at a time for 2–3 minutes, or until golden brown and crisp. Drain on absorbent kitchen paper and arrange on a warmed platter. Garnish with spring onion tassels and serve immediately.

Try this: FOR AN ALTERNATIVE: 200 FOR ENTERTAINING: 250

Savoury Wontons

MAKES 15

125 g/4 oz filo pastry or
  wonton skins
15 whole chive leaves
225 g/8 oz spinach
25 g/1 oz butter
½ tsp salt
225 g/8 oz mushrooms,
  wiped and roughly

chopped
1 garlic clove, peeled
  and crushed
1–2 tbsp dark soy sauce
2.5 cm/1 inch piece fresh
  root ginger, peeled
  and grated
salt and freshly ground

black pepper
1 small egg, beaten
300 ml/½ pint groundnut
  oil for deep-frying

To garnish:
spring onion curls
radish roses

Cut the filo pastry or wonton skins into 12.5 cm/5 inch squares, stack and cover with clingfilm. Chill in the refrigerator while preparing the filling. Blanch the chive leaves in boiling water for 1 minute, drain and reserve.

Melt the butter in a saucepan, add the spinach and salt and cook for 2–3 minutes or until wilted. Add the mushrooms and garlic and cook for 2–3 minutes or until tender. Transfer the spinach and mushroom mixture to a bowl. Stir in the soy sauce and ginger. Season to taste with salt and pepper.

Place a small spoonful of the spinach and mushroom mixture on to a pastry or wonton square and brush the edges with beaten egg. Gather up the four corners to make a little bag and tie with a chive leaf. Make up the remainder of the wontons.

Heat a wok, add the oil and heat to 180°C/350°F. Deep-fry the wontons in batches for 2–3 minutes, or until golden and crisp. Drain on absorbent kitchen paper and serve immediately, garnished with spring onion curls and radish roses.

Try this: FOR AN ALTERNATIVE: 186 FOR ENTERTAINING: 242

Cooked Vegetable Salad with Satay Sauce

SERVES 4

125 ml/4 fl oz groundnut oil
225 g/8 oz unsalted peanuts
1 onion, peeled and
    finely chopped
1 garlic clove, peeled
    and crushed
½ tsp chilli powder
1 tsp ground coriander
½ tsp ground cumin
½ tsp sugar

1 tbsp dark soy sauce
2 tbsp fresh lemon juice
2 tbsp light olive oil
salt and freshly ground
    black pepper
125 g/4 oz French
    green beans, trimmed
    and halved
125 g/4 oz carrots
125 g/4 oz cauliflower florets

125 g/4 oz broccoli florets
125 g/4 oz Chinese leaves
    or pak choi, trimmed
    and shredded
125 g/4 oz beansprouts
1 tbsp sesame oil

To garnish:
sprigs of fresh watercress
cucumber, cut into slivers

Heat a wok, add the oil, and when hot, add the peanuts and stir-fry for 3–4 minutes. Drain on absorbent kitchen paper and leave to cool. Blend in a food processor to a fine powder.

Place the onion and garlic, with the spices, sugar, soy sauce, lemon juice and olive oil in a food processor. Season to taste with salt and pepper, then process into a paste. Transfer to a wok and stir-fry for 3–4 minutes.

Stir 600 ml/1 pint hot water into the paste and bring to the boil. Add the ground peanuts and simmer gently for 5–6 minutes or until the mixture thickens. Reserve the satay sauce.

Cook in batches in lightly salted boiling water. Cook the French beans, carrots, cauliflower and broccoli for 3–4 minutes, and the Chinese leaves or pak choi and beansprouts for 2 minutes. Drain each batch, drizzle over the sesame oil and arrange on a large warmed serving dish. Garnish with watercress sprigs and cucumber. Serve with the satay sauce.

Try this: FOR AN ALTERNATIVE: 254 FOR ENTERTAINING: 152

Index